W.D. Snodgrass

in conversation
with

Philip Hoy

W.D. Snodgrass

in conversation
with

Philip Hoy

Between
The
Lines

First published in 1998 by

Between The Lines

9 Woodstock Road
London N4 3ET
UK

Copyright © Philip Hoy 1998
The right of Philip Hoy to be identified
as the author of this work has been asserted
by him in accordance with the Copyright,
Designs and Patents Act of 1988.
All rights reserved.

A CIP catalogue record for this book
is available from the British Library.

ISBN 0 9532841 0 7

Printed and Bound by

The Ipswich Book Company Ltd.,
The Drift,
Nacton Road,
Ipswich,
Suffolk IP3 9QR,
UK.

Between The Lines

Editorial Board

Peter Dale – Ian Hamilton – Philip Hoy

This imprint is devoted to publishing more than usually wide-ranging, and more than usually deep-going, interviews with some of today's most accomplished poets.

Some would deny that any useful purpose is served by putting questions to a writer which are not answered by his or her books. For them, what Yeats called 'the bundle of accident and incoherence that sits down to breakfast' is best left alone, not asked to interrupt its cornflakes, or to set aside its morning paper, while someone with a tape-recorder inquires about its life, habits and attitudes.

If we do not share this view, it is not because we endorse Sainte-Beuve's dictum, *tel arbre, tel fruit* – *as the tree, so the fruit* – but because we understand what Geoffrey Braithwaite was getting at when the author of *Flaubert's Parrot* had him say:

> 'But if you love a writer, if you depend upon the drip-feed of his intelligence, if you want to pursue him and find him – despite edicts to the contrary – then it's impossible to know too much.'

Forthcoming volumes will feature **Donald Hall, Hans Magnus Enzensberger, Michael Hamburger, Anthony Hecht, Anthony Thwaite and Richard Wilbur**, figures who have established reputations not just as poets, but as translators, editors, essayists and/or critics as well.

Besides the interview, each volume will contain a sketch of the poet's life and career, a comprehensive bibliography, archival information, and a representative selection of quotations from the poet's critics and reviewers. It is hoped that the results will be of interest to the lay reader and specialist alike.

Contents

A Note on W.D. Snodgrass	11
A Note on Philip Hoy	15
The Conversation	17
Bibliography	59
The Critics	75

A Note on W.D. Snodgrass

W.D. Snodgrass was born in Wilkinsburg, Pennsylvania, in 1926, and was educated at Geneva College. His studies were interrupted when, during WWII, he was drafted into the Navy, and sent to the Pacific.

After demobilization, Snodgrass resumed his studies, but transferred from Geneva College to the University of Iowa, eventually enrolling in the Iowa Writers' Workshop, which had been established in 1937, and was attracting as tutors some of the finest poetic talents of the day, amongst them John Berryman, Randall Jarrell and Robert Lowell.

Snodgrass's first poems appeared in 1951, and throughout the 1950's he published in some of the most prestigious magazines (e.g. *Botteghe Oscure, Partisan Review, The New Yorker, The Paris Review* and *The Hudson Review*). However, in 1957, five sections from a sequence entitled 'Heart's Needle' were included in Hall, Pack and Simpson's anthology, *New Poets of England and America*, and these were to mark a turning-point. When Lowell had been shown early versions of these poems, in 1953, he had disliked them, but now he was full of admiration. He wrote to Elizabeth Bishop, saying:

> 'I must tell you that I've discovered a new poet, W.D. Snodgrass – he was once one of my Iowa students, and I merely thought him about the best. Now he turns out to be better than anyone except Larkin.'[1]

He also wrote to Randall Jarrell, this time calling Snodgrass Larkin's equal, and comparing him to the great French poet, Jules Laforgue.[2] The point was developed in an interview he gave *The Paris Review* rather later:

> 'I think a lot of the best poetry is [on the verge of being slight and sentimental]. Laforgue – it's hard to think of a more delightful poet ... Well, it's on the verge of being sentimental, and if he hadn't dared to be sentimental he wouldn't have been a poet. I mean, his inspiration was that. There's some way of distinguishing between

---

[1] Lowell to Bishop, 29 April 1957, Vassar College Library Special Collections, Poughkeepsie, New York.

[2] Lowell to Jarrell, 24 October 1957, The Henry W. and Albert A. Berg Collection, New York Public Library, Lenox and Tilden Foundation, New York.

false sentimentality, which is blowing up a subject and giving emotions that you don't feel, and using whimsical, minute, tender, small emotions that most people don't feel but which Laforgue and Snodgrass do. So that I'd say he [Snodgrass] had pathos and fragility ... He has fragility along the edges and a main artery of power going through the center.'[3]

As well as writing to Bishop and Jarrell, Lowell wrote to Snodgrass, saying how much he admired the anthologized poems, and offering to help him find a book publisher.

By the time *Heart's Needle* was published, in 1959, Snodgrass had already won the *The Hudson Review* Fellowship in Poetry and an Ingram Merrill Foundation Poetry Prize. However, his first book brought him something more: a citation from the Poetry Society of America, a grant from the National Institute of Arts, and, most important of all, 1960's Pulitzer Prize in Poetry.

It is often said that *Heart's Needle* inaugurated *confessional* verse. Snodgrass dislikes the term, and is quick to point out that the kind of verse he was writing at that time – a 'searingly personal' verse, as Ann Sexton called it – was hardly unprecedented. This is true, but it is also true that the genre he was reviving here seemed revolutionary to most of his contemporaries, reared as they had been on the anti-expressionistic principles of the New Critics.

Snodgrass's confessional work was to have a profound effect on many of his contemporaries, amongst them, and most importantly, Robert Lowell. The evidence for this is on display in Lowell's most accomplished volume, *Life Studies*, which appeared in the same year as *Heart's Needle*, and enabled its author to carry off the other great literary prize for 1960, the National Book Award.[4] The effect on other poets, on both sides of the At-

---

[3] Frederick Seidel: 'The Art of Poetry: Robert Lowell', in *Robert Lowell: Interviews and Memoirs*, ed. Jeffrey Meyers, University of Michigan Press, Ann Arbor, 1988, 56; first published in *The Paris Review* 7, Winter-Spring 1961, 59-65.

[4] For many years, it was assumed that Snodgrass had been following in Lowell's footsteps, but as has already been pointed out, Lowell was shown versions of the 'Heart's Needle' poems as early as 1953, four years before his own work took a confessional turn. Some might nevertheless resist the idea that the teacher was following in his student's footsteps, pointing out, for example, that, in the letter he sent Snodgrass in 1957, Lowell acknowledged having found his way to *Life Studies* after Snodgrass had found his way to 'Heart's Needle', but in words which do not allow us to conclude that 'Heart's Needle' had shown him the way: 'I have been working very hard myself lately and have written almost half a book since the middle of August, and feel I have just really begun to know how to get out

lantic, is fairly described as *liberating*. As one English critic was to put it later on:

> '"Confessional" was an unfortunate way of describing what was new about *Life Studies* and *Heart's Needle* – the term reeks of guilt and ingratiation – but it does recall the general surprise that such poetic vibrance and composure could be won from subjects that seemed doomed to privacy or narcissistic inflation.'[5]

In the almost forty years since this auspicious debut, Snodgrass has gone on to produce an impressively diverse body of work, including *After Experience, Remains, A Locked House, W.D.'s Midnight Carnival, The Death of Cock Robin, Each in His Season, The Führer Bunker*, seven volumes of translations, and a large number of essays too, some of which were collected in *In Radical Pursuit*. These books have seriously divided the critics, bringing bouquets from some and brickbats from others. Most controversial of all was *The Führer Bunker*, a book which not only pitted critics against each other, but in one notable case pitted a critic against himself.[6]

Snodgrass has a long and distinguished academic career behind him, having taught at Cornell, Rochester, Wayne State, Syracuse, Old Dominion, and Delaware Universities. He retired from teaching in 1994, and now devotes himself full-time to his writing. He lives with his 'fourth, last and best' wife, the writer, Kathleen Snodgrass (née Browne), spending six months of each year at their home in New York, and the other six months in Mexico.

---

what I want to say, what I've lived. You learned earlier.' Later on, in 1961, Lowell came closer to acknowledging Snodgrass's influence, telling Frederick Seidel, in the interview from which we have already quoted: 'He did these things before I did, though he's younger than I am and had been my student. He may have influenced me, though people have suggested the opposite' (*Robert Lowell: Interviews and Memoirs*, 56). There is no proof to be had here, but what is it easier to accept – that Lowell found no encouragement for his own confessional work in the confessional work of Snodgrass, or that what Bloom calls the *anxiety of influence* made it hard for him to come right out and acknowledge the fact?

[5] Ian Hamilton, *A Poetry Chronicle*, Faber and Faber, London, 1973, 174.

[6] See Larry Levis, 'Not Life So Proud To Be Life: Snodgrass, Rothenberg, Bell and the Counter-Revolution', and the same author's 'Waiting for the End of the World: Snodgrass and *The Fuehrer Bunker*', in ed. Stephen Haven, *The Poetry of W.D. Snodgrass: Everything Human*, University of Michigan Press, Ann Arbor, MI, 1993.

A Note on Philip Hoy

Philip Hoy was born in London in 1952. He has a Ph.D in Philosophy, and has taught that subject for many years, here in the UK, but most recently overseas.

Amongst Hoy's most recent publications are: '"The Starry Night": Snodgrass's Van Gogh Reconsidered' (*Agenda*, 1996), 'The Genesis of *On Certainty*: Some Questions for Professors Anscombe and von Wright' (*Wittgenstein Studies*, University of Passau, 1996), the proem and afterword to Peter Dale's latest book, *Da Capo* (Agenda Editions, 1997), and '*The Will to Power* #486/KGW VIII, 1 2[87], 2: A Knot that Won't Unravel?' (*Nietzsche Studien*, Walter de Gruyter, Berlin, 1998).

After returning to the UK in 1996, Hoy settled in north London, where he is writing a critical study of the poetry of W.D. Snodgrass – *The Heart's Trapeze* – as well as sitting on the editorial board of *Between the Lines*. He lives with the Italian architect, Evelina Francia.

A Conversation with W.D. Snodgrass

What follows is the edited transcript of a conversation which was recorded at the remote farmhouse in upstate New York where W.D. Snodgrass lives with his wife, Kathy, and their lively dog, Sasha. It was conducted over the space of four days, between June 12th and June 16th, 1997.

On the first and last day, we were able to sit in the garden, soaking up the sunshine and pausing only to marvel at the humming-birds, phoebes and blue-jays which took it in turns to distract us. But rain drove us indoors the rest of the time, and there we sat in the living-room, surrounded by the Snodgrasses' musical instruments – a piano, a harpsichord, a ten-string guitar, a cister, and an oud – papier-mâché sculptures from Mexico, folk-paintings from Eastern Europe, some of the poet's own broadsides, framed and mounted, and a handful of works by his collaborator, the artist, DeLoss McGraw, amongst them a striking statuette of their joint creation, Mr Evil. Even indoors, the humming-birds continued to be a distraction, as they dived to, hovered at, and then flew off from the feeders hanging outside the windows, but a greater distraction here proved to be Sasha, the dog who, if he hadn't been so young, and only recently acquired, might have been thought the model for Mr Evil!

I'd like to begin by asking you a few questions about your days as a student in the creative writing classes at The University of Iowa. Paul Engle was the man behind the program, as I understand it.

They already had a creative writing program before he got involved. He'd made a big name early in his life by writing some fairly bad poems, but then he took over the program, built it up, and turned it into something very important. At least half of the people of my generation who were going to become any good as writers were students there.

The list is very impressive: Henri Coulette, Robert Dana, Jane Cooper, William Dickey, Shirley Eliason, Donald Justice, Philip Levine, Donald Petersen, William Stafford ...

And then there were the people who *taught* there! Engle himself could be a brilliant teacher. I remember him introducing us to Baudelaire, Verlaine and Rimbaud, and making us see ways of meaning we'd never even thought of. Ruthven Todd was there in my first year, and later on there was Reed Whittemore, Karl Shapiro, Robert Lowell, John Berryman. Then there were the people who came for shorter periods: Robert Penn Warren,

Cleanth Brooks, Allen Tate, John Crowe Ransom, John Ciardi, Dylan Thomas, Randall Jarrell …

That's quite a roll call!

The creative writing classes were *unbelievable*. Those people knew what they were talking about, and they cared. Most of them, at any rate.

But Lowell is quoted on the dust-jacket of Heart's Needle *as saying, 'He [Snodgrass] flowered in the most sterile of sterile places, a post war, cold war Midwestern university's poetry workshop for graduate students.' Why do you think he was so scathing about the place?*

I've no idea! If he thought so badly of it, why did he spend so much time there? But he could sometimes hold outrageous opinions – and with great energy.

What were your earliest poems like?

I was writing under the influence of William Empson. I'd fallen for that intense, and very intellectual, style. I wrote several villanelles during that period. After that, I discovered Robert Lowell. *Lord Weary's Castle* had just won the Pulitzer Prize, and those poems were something new, something different. I may not have *understood* them, but I was *overwhelmed* by them!

Was this before or after Lowell had started teaching at Iowa?

Oh, before.

And after his arrival, what sort of impression did he make on you? Did he live up to your expectations?

I thought he was marvellous. He came for a semester over the space of several years, and usually he'd run a course on the masterpieces of English poetry as well as giving a series of workshops. I was absolutely exhausted by the torrent of ideas, but also wonderfully invigorated by the brilliance of his perceptions.

Philip Levine told Paul Mariani that he was deeply disappointed by Lowell, that Lowell only had time for his favourites, and was visibly bored by the others – him-

self included.

I didn't know that at the time, and don't know anyone else who felt that way.

What sorts of poems were you producing while under Lowell's influence?

Oh, highly intellectual, highly rhetorical poems, with brilliant textures and driving rhythms ...

You don't sound very enthusiastic about them.

They lacked any real intensity or passion. This was something I realized when I heard the great Swiss tenor Hugues Cuenod for the first time. The radio was playing his *Spanish and Italian Songs of the 16th and 17th centuries.* Do you know them?

I'm afraid I don't.

They're just incredible. They had everything my poems lacked.

Was it this experience which helped move you to find your own voice, the voice we associate with Heart's Needle?

That was one of them.

What were the others?

Well, I went to a writer's conference in Boulder, Colorado, and met Randall Jarrell. After looking at some of the poems I'd given him – poems which Warren, Ransom and the others had liked – he said, 'Snodgrass, you're writing the very best second-rate Lowell in the whole country!'

It could have been a lot worse. Coming from Jarrell, I mean!

He didn't care for the high-flown language, the pretension. 'What are you trying to do,' he said, 'turn yourself into a fireworks factory?' But I'd also given him a couple of translations – one from Ovid, the other from Rilke – and these he *did* like. I'd regarded them as exercises, but they made sense to him, I suppose because of their emotional directness. After that, he told me to go and have a look at another poem of Rilke's, the wonderful 'Orpheus, Eurydice, Hermes'. Towards the end of the poem, Hermes realizes that Orpheus has disobeyed the instruction not to look back, and cries out: 'Oh, but he is looking at us!' Eurydice then says something that absolutely takes your breath away: 'Wer?' – 'Who?' She has no idea who Orpheus is! It's an incredible moment. Jarrell said, 'What can you do with fancy language that's going to match the invention of that?'

There was also the collapse of my first marriage. I was desperate about not being able to see my daughter. For two whole years, I wasn't able to write anything. Finally, I went into psychotherapy, which showed me that the problem wouldn't go away while I went on talking about it in fancy psychological language. I had to get away from that, to start talking about the problem in my own voice.

I gather your fellow student, Robert Shelley, may also have helped you to change direction?

Yes. He'd been writing imitations of Hart Crane. Then, one day, he called me, wanting to read out something he'd just finished. It was simple, direct, lyrical – all the things our teachers had said were no longer possible – and it knocked me over. I remember saying, 'That's it – you've got it!' As you probably know, he committed suicide not long after that. It was a terrible waste.

If Jarrell's name comes up these days, it's likely to be in connection with his criticism, or, just possibly, the novel. Apart from things like 'The Ball Turret Gunner' and 'The Woman at the Washington Zoo', his poems are almost completely forgotten. How do you feel about that?

I think it's a great shame. I think very highly of his poems, many of them. They move me more than Lowell's. And more often than Lowell's.

How do you explain the neglect?

The main reason Jarrell's poems aren't known better is that he reviewed Oscar Williams's *Treasury of Modern Poetry* saying, roughly, *It takes great self-confidence to like your own poems seven times better than Whitman's, six times better than Hardy's, etc.* The very next printing, Jarrell found a copy of the book in his mailbox with a marker where his poems *had* been. Ironically, Williams went on including Jarrell's choice of poems by both Whitman and Hardy, who, largely because of Eliot, were in terrible disrepute then. So, indirectly, Jarrell reinstated both those marvellous poets. *Himself* he could not save.

I wonder whether that Wildean line of Vendler's, about Jarrell putting his talent into his poetry and his genius into his criticism didn't also take root in people's minds?

Well, he was one of our best critics, one of the people you ought to read if you're at all interested in literature. There aren't too many people you can say that of. Donald Hall's an admirable exception, and there may be one or two others. But on the whole, today's critics are more concerned about their careers and empire-building ...

I was re-reading Dana Gioia's book, Can Poetry Matter, *on the way over, and he says much the same ...*

It's about the one thing in that book I can agree with! – But to go back to Jarrell for a moment. He was a great teacher. We thought we knew what Prufrock was all about, because all the critics and all the teachers told us it was about Eliot's move towards religion. Then Jarrell went through it with us, and it was like reading it for the first time. How had we overlooked the lady, or not understood Prufrock's urge to 'go through certain half-deserted streets' to ask her 'an overwhelming question'?

On another occasion, he spent an hour talking about the ballad 'Frankie and Johnny'. Nobody else would have spent two minutes on it, but by the end of that hour, we had to agree that this is one of the best poems to have come out of America.

I mentioned Helen Vendler a moment ago. Do you have any explanation of why it is that your name is never mentioned in any of the many books she's published?

I guess she just doesn't like what I write.

But even if she thought you a minor talent, that wouldn't explain your complete absence from her books. After all, she's written a great deal about people like Lowell and Sexton, poets, that's to say, who not only rated you very highly, but who were clearly influenced by your work. To discuss them without even so much as mentioning you is either the result of rotten scholarship or else the result of something having nothing to do with scholarship.

I'd lean toward the latter. The only time I met her, Vendler's coldness suggested some personal dislike. But I shouldn't hazard guesses about why. Or even whether.

John Berryman was another of the figures you got to know in Iowa. What sort of impression did he make on you? Was he an impressive teacher?

Well, he was only there for one semester, and I could only get to an occasional class. As well as fighting to see my child, I was working as an aide in a hospital, so I didn't have much time left. But he *was* a very impressive teacher, and very different from anyone else I had had. I didn't always understand what he was saying. I couldn't work out what principles lay behind his judgements, couldn't even be sure that there were any such principles. But he was full of startling insights, and we learnt a lot. I remember him going through 'Song of Myself', and at one point looking up and saying, 'You know what that proves? That proves most people can't write poetry!'

The best things were the writing classes. On one occasion, Donald Justice handed in a sonnet – it was about the angels driving Adam and Eve out of Paradise – and after he'd read it through, Berryman said, 'It's just not right, to get a poem like that as a classroom assignment!'

If that's the poem I'm thinking of, it's in his Selected. *It's called 'The Wall,' or something like that.*

My own poem, 'A Flat One', was written as a result of Berryman's asking us to write a stanzaic poem about a death. I wrote about one of the patients at the hospital I was working in, something it wouldn't have occurred to me to do without that assignment. It had to be revised later, but I've always been grateful to Berryman for having made that poem possible.

You came to be a great admirer of Berryman's poetry, didn't you? According to Lowell, you left a reading of the Dream Songs *Berryman gave in 1962 saying, 'There's no point anybody else writing any more.'*

That was at the National Poetry Festival, in the Library of Congress in Washington – a deeply depressing affair. Randall and Mary Jarrell were there, and on seeing a BBC reporter making her way to one of the worst meetings, equipped with a Nagra tape recorder, he said to me, 'We'll grab *her.* You take the *recorder.* No evidence of this must ever get out of the country!'

Well, Berryman gave the first public reading of his *Dream Songs* at that Festival, and boy! Talk about a good deed in a naughty world! Everyone was overwhelmed – even Allen Tate. He wasn't in the habit of applauding other people's work, but that day he was shouting, 'Bravo, John!'

What was it about those early Dream Songs *that so impressed you?*

Before going to Washington, I'd read some of them, but I hadn't understood them. I don't think I made much of an effort to understand them, because, reading them silently, I'd not grasped the vitality, the drama. But then, when John read them out loud, all of that was suddenly obvious, and the audience was *electrified*. Of course, there was still a lot I didn't understand, but the confidence with which he read the lines left you in no doubt that they were understandable, and now you wanted to understand.

But your fondness for the early Dream Songs *doesn't extend to the ones he wrote later, as I understand it?*

Right. As time went on, he kept trying to do the same thing, and in my opinion it wore a little thin. Some of the later ones work, but not many, and none are as utterly unpredictable as those early ones, with lines as improbable as, 'Often he reckons, in the dawn, them up'!

'and somehow a dog/has taken itself & its tail considerably away/into mountains or sea or sky, leaving/ behind: me, wag'!

Right.

You mentioned William Empson at the start of this interview. Did you ever meet the man?

I did, but not until the 1970's. He'd been living in retirement, but came out of it because England's economy was in a bad way. He came to the University of Delaware, where I was teaching, and I met him at a party. He wasn't what I had been expecting. That beard of his was gone, he wasn't smoking a pipe and a cigarette at the same time …

A pipe and a cigarette at the same time!?

You didn't know about that?

No.

There's a wonderful story about it. Apparently, one of Empson's students got up the courage one day, and said, 'Professor Empson, do you mind if I ask you why you do that?' Empson was momentarily thrown, but quickly recovered himself, and said, 'Oh, that's easy: I started smoking cigarettes while I was an undergraduate, but then I went to China, where they didn't have cigarettes, and that's when I took up the pipe.'

And that was it?

That was it!

The student should have known better, putting a question like that to the author of The Seven Types!

With him at the party was his wife, a much younger woman, who treated him and everyone else with absolute contempt. I told her at one point how much I'd wanted to meet her husband, and do you know what she said? 'You *may* have been in time.'
   He *was* rather a sad figure by this time. When I told him how much his poems had meant to me, he didn't seem to understand what I was saying. We happened to leave the party at the same time, and I remember him hurrying across the lawn to catch up with his wife and another man. It was raining, and she was shouting, 'Bill! Bill! Get off that grass! You'll catch your death of cold! Have you no sense!?' It was said that the other man was her lover, and that Empson used to take them their breakfast every morning.

You were a teacher yourself for many years, only retiring in 1994. Did your style as a teacher owe anything to the styles of your own teachers?

I'm sure it did, though it might not be easy to say what was owed to Engle, what was owed to Lowell, and so on. I was very slow in returning my students' work, and didn't always do *their* poems in class, and I could try blaming Jarrell for that. He infuriated the students at that writers' conference by talking about 'Prufrock', or 'Frankie and Johnny', instead of *their* poems.

One thing I did which none of my teachers had done was to *un*-write certain poems, that's to say, to take a good poem and then write a bad version of it. An example would be Hardy's 'Transformations', and my version of it, 'Resurrections'. The second stanza of his goes like this:

> These grasses must be made
> Of her who often prayed,
> Last century, for repose;
> And the fair girl long ago
> Whom I often tried to know
> May be entering this rose.

The second stanza of mine goes like this:

> These grasses must be she
> Who prayed, last century,
> For peace after life's woes;
> And the girl, fair and sweet,
> I had often tried to meet
> Glows, warmly, in this rose.

I did a lot of that kind of thing, not only because it was useful in class, but because it gave me the pleasure of revenge on people who wrote better than I could! *De/Compositions*, I call them, and I'm thinking of putting them together as a book. – But maybe this technique wasn't unrelated to something Lowell did in one of his classes, when he talked about the two versions of Wyatt's poem, 'They flee from me' -

You mean Wyatt's original and Tottel's regularized version?

That's right.

It's a remarkable poem.

It sure is, and it meant a great deal to Lowell, as it did to his teacher, Allen Tate. Tate taught it to him just as he taught it to us, and it influenced both of them, I think.

Oh?

What they liked was the quality of its rhetoric. But neither of them could achieve the straightforward, unvarnished quality of 'It was no dream: I lay broad waking'. Lowell found it in his best poems but got distracted, as Tate almost always did, by a yearning to be big and sound important.

But now I come to think of it, that technique of De/Composing may also be related to what other of my teachers did when they looked at Pope's versions of earlier poems.

Was it a wrench, giving up teaching back in 94?

No, it was a welcome release. I enjoyed being inside a University community, but I didn't much like the teaching. I miss some things, of course. I used to give courses in reading poetry out loud, and they were a lot of fun. But the courses in writing poetry, *those* I don't miss at all. I was always enraging the students because I kept their work for so long. It took a lot of energy, trying to understand what was going through a student's mind, trying to work out why they were using this kind of language rather than that, so I'd want to go on reading their poems for as long as I could ... And all the time, I was terrified I was going to do some harm.

What was it about the reading classes you so enjoyed?

Oral interpretation is a subject that *can* be taught, and I knew how to teach it. The students would love those classes, and within six weeks they were delighted with what they became able to do. We got to talk about aspects of a poem that wouldn't get discussed in regular literary classes, with a lot of time looking at the nature of the emotion, how it developed or changed, and so on. In talking about how to bring all this out, I got quite close to those students, closer than to most of the others.

You said you enjoyed being inside a University community, even if you didn't much care for the teaching, most of it. What was it that appealed to you?

Excellence isn't rewarded in the Universities, but it isn't punished as often as it is in many other places. And of course a University does offer you people you can talk to.

Does, or did? *Only, writing about your days at Iowa, you recently said, 'One never doubted, as so often since, that one belonged to a genuine University community, a body of scholars, critics and writers who, even when dead wrong, truly cared about their subjects.'*

Well, our universities aren't what they were. There are many of them, and many more students. And they're at the scant mercy of too many pressure groups. If it's not the communists, it's the anti-communists. Or the feminists. Or the multi-culturalists. Or the fundamentalists. Who has time or energy left to think about excellence? That's part of the unrecognized intent of most such groups.

Apart from giving you the subject matter of a few poems, did being a teacher influence your writing in any way?

Would I have done things differently if I'd become an accountant? Apart from writing the occasional poem about ledger books?! I don't know …

Since your retirement as a teacher, you've been a full-time writer. What is your typical working day, if you have such a thing?

In a sense I do, although I don't always stick to it. I try to write in the morning, but by the afternoon I'm likely to be feeling discontented, so I find an excuse to go out, perhaps for a walk, or maybe to one of the towns round here. Evenings I try to write letters, but I don't often succeed. Mostly I'll listen to music, or watch a basket-ball game …
   That probably doesn't sound very organized, but this is much more organized than I've been most of my life. I once thought I'd become a librarian, and talked to the lady who directed the most prestigious library school. After five minutes of conversation, she arose and announced: 'Mr Snodgrass, I am afraid you do not have an orderly mind!' – What acuity!

How do you account for this disorderliness?

I was one of those babies they put on two-hour schedules: you had to eat every two hours, poop every two hours, sleep every two hours… After that, inevitably, I spent most of my life *breaking* schedules. I never wrote poems unless I was supposed to be studying for an examination, or something like that. I remember, a psychiatrist I went to see asked me about my work-schedule, and I said, 'I don't have any.' And he said, 'Oh, no, no, no – of course you have a schedule, it's just an irregular one.' And I had to insist, 'No, really, I don't have any.' That doesn't mean I wasn't making schedules. I'd *make* them alright, but then I'd forget about them, or find some reason for ignoring them. I do the same thing with filing systems – you know, starting one before finishing with another. I've managed to lose all sorts of things like that, poems and especially translations.

What about the mechanics of writing? Do you use a word-processor?

For prose, certainly. For poems, I work with a pen, at least through four or five drafts, then I'll transfer it to the screen.

Why the difference?

I've no idea! Poems come slower, I guess. But that's not always true. No, I don't know why!

Do poems have anything like a normal gestation period?

I used to think I was slower than anyone I'd ever known. I mean, I worked on *The Führer Bunker* for maybe thirty-five years!

But that's a complete cycle, of, what, eighty poems?

Alright, but individual poems have sometimes taken me eight to ten years to finish. That might be unusual, but it never surprised me. More recently, when I got mixed up with the painter Deloss McGraw, and the challenge of his unbelievable fertility, I was turning out poems pretty fast. They were a different kind of poem, with a much lighter, more comical surface, but still, this was totally unexpected, a nice surprise.

How quickly were you be able to produce a poem when working with McGraw?

Let's see. We were going to do an alphabet together. I went down to Mexico one year – Kathy and I spend our winters down there, as you know – and I decided I would do a poem for each letter of the alphabet, trying to produce one a day …

These were the poems that appear in your Selected *as 'A Darkling Alphabet'?*

Yes. Towards the end, I was doing two or three a day. And on the last day, I managed *five!* I couldn't believe it. Nothing's gone that easy since. But as a matter of fact, since finishing *The Führer Bunker*, I've hardly written any poems.

But that book only came out a couple of years ago.

Well, since then I've written five short poems for a cycle called *Nocturnes*, and another poem entitled 'Lifelong', which was for two friends of ours in Mexico, who got married when it became obvious that he was dying. But that's about it.

Those are the poems that were published in the issue of Agenda *which was recently devoted to your work?*

That's right.

How much revising do you do, typically?

It used to be that, if I got done writing a poem without having pages *that* thick, I thought I was very lucky. But as I said, the things I did with Del McGraw would be produced with very little in the way of revision.

How quickly do you send things off for publication? Do you send them off as soon as you think you're finished, or do you put them in a drawer for a while, to see how they look after you've taken a break?

I rarely send things straight off. I like to show them to friends first. But I do also want to see how they'll look when they've cooled.

My wives were always the first to see what I'd done, even when they had no literary background. Then, for many years, I'd ask George Elliott what he thought. Now, I go to another old friend, Don Hall. I haven't always acted on my friends' advice, but neither have I ever rushed to the conclusion that they were wrong.

Did you ever regret having something published?

Not that I recall. Some people say that once a poem's in print, it shouldn't be revised. That's never been my view. There were times when a magazine asked me to make changes, and if I wanted to appear there very badly, I'd make them, and figure, 'I can always change it back again later.'

The New Yorker did that a few times, and I went along with it, because they had such a wide readership, and because they paid so well! Of course, I didn't do that where I thought the changes were really damaging, or couldn't be reversed later.

Do I take it, then, that when we get to see your Collected Poems, *all of the pieces omitted from your* Selected – *there were quite a few one missed, especially from* After Experience – *that all will be restored, that none have been disowned?*

I thought then that what was left out would appear in a larger *Selected*, but there probably won't be one ...

Oh?

James Fenton was hoping to put one together in England. He came to stay with us a few years ago, and the two of us had it all worked out. Later we heard that there were going to be problems with copyright, so it came to nothing.

That's a great pity, because your things are so scattered. Fenton says in the essay he wrote about you for Agenda *that, to keep up with your work, one would have had to be not just an attentive reader, and a bibliophile, but a bit of a detective too. If anything, I think he was understating the difficulties!*

It *is* a pity, but this won't be the first thing I haven't been able to get published.

What else won't we get to see?

I've worked on a number of projects which nobody would touch. The one I'm most sorry about came out of a trip Kathy and I made to Romania in the early '80s. We came across an astonishing graveyard in a place called Sapinta. At the head of each grave we found a beautiful wooden monument. These were carved and decorated by a local man, who included a short verse epitaph, giving the dead person's name and back-ground, and then pronouncing on their character, praising them for their honesty, damning them for their laziness ... No-one got to be buried there whose family wasn't prepared to let this guy have his say. We took a lot of photos, and I made translations of all the epitaphs, but as I say, no-one would publish the result.

Perhaps what puts them off is the cost of reproducing all those photos?

That may have something to do with it. I've translated many many many troubadour songs, and I've only been able to publish a small number, because publishers can't afford to print the music that goes with them.

But you know, I've been out of favour with the literary establishment in recent years, and my work isn't sought after as it once was. But hey, I shouldn't complain too much. I've been able to do the projects I wanted to do, even if I couldn't see all of them published.

What other things of yours are we unlikely to see?

Well, let's see. I translated Max Frisch's *Biedermann and the Firebugs*, and only saw that performed in two college productions, because rights had been given to a theatre personality, someone who actually scorned Frisch and his work. His version was so thin and watery that productions had to be tricked up with junky songs and stage claptrap.

But if we look at what you have *been able to publish, it's no small amount. By my count, you have nine books of poetry, two books of translations, a book of essays, and any number of limited fine press editions to your credit. Gone are the days when your output could be described as* modest.

You're right. What *do* I have to moan about? – I still moan.

Well, it must be very frustrating if you've produced things you're pleased with, and they end up being seen only by friends, and not a wider public.

What makes it really frustrating is knowing that, if I'd not only been *nominated* for the National Book Critics' Award for Poetry, but had *won* it ...

That was for the incomplete version of The Führer Bunker, *back in 1977?*

Yes. If I'd won that award, these other things probably would have been published. I was later told that they *had* decided to give it to me, but that, when Lowell died, they decided to give it to him instead.

That was for Day for Day?

Yes.

Lowell a long way from his best.

Well, the *decision* may have been for the best. When I won the Pulitzer Prize, back in 1960, I didn't know how to handle it. I found I couldn't write, my second marriage fell apart ...

What was it William James called success? The bitch-goddess!

Well, it wasn't *all* bad! The day after I won the Pulitzer Prize, I was offered jobs by schools that wouldn't have taken me as a student the day before. It also made it possible for me to go places I would never have seen otherwise – to Eastern Europe, the Middle-East, North-Africa ...

But you know, I went through eight years of psychoanalysis, partly because of the difficulties I had then. Winning the Critics' Award might have caused me more problems, even after all that time. I tell myself that for consolation, anyway. A variation on sour grapes ...

No-one can have accused you of courting the literary establishment at that time. I mean, if you were out to win favour, there were other, more promising routes than the one you were taking, working on The Führer Bunker *cycle.*

I knew perfectly well that people were going to *hate* me for doing those poems. I didn't know *how long* they'd hate me, or *how intensely*, but yes, you're right: I wasn't seeking success. Not immediate success, anyway. On the other hand, if I knew they'd disapprove of the poems for a while, still I must have hoped they'd eventually come round and say, 'Oh, how wrong we've been! How *can* we have been so blind?!'

I'd like to ask you a few questions about The Führer Bunker, *which, in its complete form, is your most recent book-length publication. And I'd like to start with a question about its presentation. For the incomplete version you published in 1977, you wrote an afterword, which, amongst other things, sought to impress on the reader the extent to which what you had written rested on fact. So, you told us that Eva Braun really did have a fondness for the song 'Tea for Two', that Hitler really did have coprophiliac fantasies, that many of the lines you'd placed in the mouths of your characters were taken from the originals' letters, and so on. You also acknowledged, and tried to justify, some of the departures from fact that were involved, as when you had Speer quoting from writers he almost certainly didn't know at that time. Now, I don't want to take you up on any of this. I want instead to ask why it was that when you came to publish the complete cycle, back in 1995, you thought better of including this afterword, thought better of including any afterword, in fact.*

Partly because it was used to bludgeon me. Some of the people who wrote about the book misquoted things I said there, or deliberately misinterpreted them. At one point, I said that I'd had these people express thoughts and feelings they probably wouldn't have dared to express in reality, to other people, or even to themselves. Someone writing in the *Dictionary of Literary Biography* seized on that and said, 'Snodgrass admits to making the Nazis more appealing than they were,' or words to that effect. I couldn't believe it. If I ever had done such a thing, I certainly wouldn't have admitted it! What I did was the exact opposite: exposing these people for what they really were, not allowing them to be seen as they wanted to be seen. Jon Silkin saw that entry in *DLB*, and said, 'If I read that about someone, I'd never read another word the son-of-a-bitch wrote.'

Was any attempt made to get the misstatement retracted?

Twice we wrote to the *DLB*, asking that something be done. We even threatened legal action. They wrote back promising to correct it, but have not done so. Perhaps I should be more combative, or maybe less cowardly …

That piece was full of errors. It said I was raised in a Quaker family. The hell I was! I became a Quaker for a short time, when I was a student, but that was it.

I'm still not sure I understand the decision to cut the afterword. I mean, some people are going to get you wrong no matter what you do, and if you'd suppressed everything that was liable to be misunderstood or misrepresented, wouldn't the whole cycle be gathering dust somewhere inside those filing-systems of yours?

Hah!

I think that afterword served a very useful purpose in orienting the reader, and I was very surprised, and not a little disappointed, when I saw that you'd decided to dispense with any such thing in the '95 edition.

Well, I talked this over with Al Poulin, of BOA, who published both voluumes, and we came to the conclusion that it wasn't possible to write anything that didn't seem like a defence. We didn't want it to seem like I was defending what I'd done.

The Führer Bunker has attracted a lot of criticism ...

You can say that again!

And some of that criticism has come from erstwhile admirers. A critic like J.D. McClatchy, for example, who demonstrated great sensitivity towards, and appreciation of, your earlier volumes, was pretty dismissive of it ...

I know he doesn't care for some of my more recent work, but has he written something about the *Bunker*?

Not at any length, but let me quote from the tail end of what little he does say: 'Turning to The Führer Bunker *[after having read* Heart's Needle, After Experience *and* Remains] *is not unlike the experience, after having read Hardy's exquisite lyrics to his dead wife, of then turning to read* The Dynasts.'

Ouch! – Well, first, I'm glad to be compared to Hardy in any case, and there *are* some points to the comparison. Still, whatever the faults of the *Bunker*, I don't think it shares those of *The Dynasts*, which is almost the only piece of Hardy's I don't like. It surely hasn't the dreary sameness of the heavily Shakespearean language. I set out using different verse forms just to catch the personal language of different specific minds.

McClatchy isn't the only admirer of yours to have found himself out of sympathy with The Führer Bunker. *There are a number of others, and they all seem to think that you took a wrong turning, or perhaps we should say* missed *your step. So far as I can see, though, you remain unmoved by this criticism, even if some of it has hurt you. You continue to think of this cycle as your most accomplished piece of work to date.*

I do.

Of course, the cycle-in-progress did have its admirers as well as its detractors, and alongside McClatchy's comments it's maybe worth placing Harold Bloom's: 'I started reading this with anticipated dread and distaste, though with admiration for Snodgrass's audacity. His audacity is more than matched by his aston-

ishing skill in ordering his intractable material and in combining his own inventions with the verifiable details of the last days of Hitler. Granted the immense difficulties he has taken on, Snodgrass demonstrates something of the power of a contemporary equivalent of Jacobean drama at its darkest.' – All the same, I think it's true to say that the detractors outnumber the admirers.*

Well, I don't know. A lot of people – people whose opinions I value – did say lovely things about the *Bunker,* and showed that they understood what I was trying to do there, but their pieces didn't appear in any of the major places. As to the other people – well, who knows what they'll be saying in 150 years?

You know, everything I've ever written was opposed at first. The poems of *Heart's Needle,* for example. There I was talking about things you weren't supposed to talk about, and in ways you weren't supposed to talk about them. People said, 'You can't do that.' But later, they changed their minds. And that poem I mentioned earlier, 'A Flat One' – that made a lot of people pretty angry too ...

What upset them about that?

I had college professors standing up at a reading I gave saying that this was an attack on the medical profession!

Which it was, of course, though it wasn't only that. It's the mores of a culture that are under fire in that poem, not just the mores of a particular profession. And in saying that, one's still only touched on one aspect of the piece.

Of course, you were allowed to write about the Nazis. As a matter of fact, more books were being written about the Nazis than just about any other thing, except cooking and dieting! But nobody was talking about them in poems.

But you must have had other reasons for taking on the Nazis? I mean, reasons other than the fact that other poets weren't willing to.

Well, I *did* want an important subject others were ignoring. But this topic had interested me ever since the war. When I was still going to playwriting classes at the University of Iowa, I tried to write a play based on Trevor-Roper's book, *The Last Days of Hitler.* That didn't work, but I stayed interested, and later on several things happened that made me think I might take the subject up again. On one occasion, I was on a panel with various people, discussing the state of American poetry. Allen Ginsberg and Amiri Baraka started out denouncing most of it. When the moderator asked them what was so bad about American poetry, Baraka pointed at me, and said, 'He is!' Before I could think of anything to say, Ginsberg and others joined in, and I was being called a reactionary or an élitist or God knows what else.

They took you to be a mouth-piece for all the evils of contemporary American society?

Yes.

What happened next?

We took a break, and the young woman I was with advised me not to try to reply. 'They'll only shout you down, and try to make you look stupid,' she said. But I thought about it, and after we resumed I thanked my accusers for what I now suggested was a compliment. I didn't think I *had* expressed all that was wrong with American society, but I reckoned that even to give the appearance of doing that you'd have to be one hell of a poet! That answer sounded a bit smart-alecky, but afterwards I came to think that it was right.

So at one level, The Führer Bunker *represents your response to a technical challenge, the challenge of finding a voice, or a medley of voices, equal to expressing evil, evil of certain kinds, at any rate. – What about the second occasion you referred to?*

Another panel, this time with Jules Feiffer, Allan Schneider and Ralph Ellison. At one point, we were discussing the identification with evil that you sometimes find in art, and the question came up whether it would be possible to make Madam Nhu [a representative of Diem's repressive régime in South Vietnam] the subject of a tragedy. Ellison began by expressing horror at the thought, but later on, after thinking it over, he changed his mind. He said that, if he'd been in her place, raised a strict Catholic, brought up to believe the things she believed, maybe he would have done many of the same things. He hoped he wouldn't have been so cruel, but he couldn't be sure, and this made him think that there might be some value in art's trying to identify with evil. That struck me as a wonderfully humane attitude ...

'Nothing human is alien to me ...'

Exactly.

So that, at another, and profounder level, The Führer Bunker *is an attempt to come to an understanding of Hitler and his circle?*

Yes. I started out with an attitude like most Americans': how could *those* people have done those terrible things? But as time went on, and I saw the things we and our former allies were doing, and went back over the history of things we'd done, it didn't look so alien as we all claimed. Again, as I worked on the poems, I began to notice things in myself that didn't square with what I'd tried to believe about myself.

Do you think that some of the criticism the cycle has attracted may have sprung from the idea that understanding must lead on to forgiveness, so that, if we're not to forgive, we must not be able to understand?

I'm sure it did.

A lot of people do seem taken with the idea – it's to be found in Arendt's The Origins of Totalitarianism, *for example, and in the afterword to Primo Levi's* If This Is a Man *and* The Truce *– but it's surely unsound ...*

You can understand why someone did something and still want to see them punished.
 But there's a more important reason why people might dislike *The Führer Bunker*, and it goes back to what I was saying a moment ago. It's comforting to believe that the Nazis were utterly different from the rest of us, so different that we can describe them as *inhuman* – or *bestial* or *fiendish* or whatever – and so different that any attempt to understand their behaviour is bound to fail. *The Führer Bunker* assumes that this is false.

Hence the epigraph: 'Mother Teresa, asked when it was she started her work for abandoned children, replied, "On the day I discovered I had a Hitler inside me."'

Right.

37

There's a fine book by Ian Buruma called The Wages of Guilt, *in which he talks about the ways in which Germany and Japan have tried to come to terms with the outrages they committed during the '30s and '40s. And I'd like to quote from a part of the book where he seeks to explain why it is that the Nazi leaders have received so little attention from writers, fictional and non-fictional. He's talking of German writers in particular, but I think the point he makes has more general application: 'This fear of biography, in fictional or documentary form, is due possibly to an idea common in the 1960s and the 1970s - that structures and institutions, not human beings, explain the past. But it must also have something to do with the fear of identification; what Germans call* Berührungsangst, *literally the fear of making contact.' I wonder if this doesn't help to explain the difficulties some people have had with* The Führer Bunker?

I very much agree with Buruma's statement about the fear of *contact*. But even stronger, I think, is the fear of *recognition*, which is what I was talking about just now. In other words, it's not only the fear that bad luck, or bad morals, are contagious and may rub off, but also, and more importantly, the fear that the disease is general and innate. I hate to agree with the church about anything, but they were right in seeing evil as innate and universal.

Did your own experience during the war contribute to The Führer Bunker *in any way? James Fenton says in the piece he wrote for* Agenda *that you didn't have any terrible experiences at the hands of the enemy ...*

The Navy is very foolish, but not so foolish as to send me into combat! The only Japanese I got to see were prisoners.

But according to Fenton, you hated what life in the Navy involved. What did it involve, for you?

Well, let me describe an incident for you. I was a brig guard for a time, and one of the prisoners we had was a huge black guy – we nicknamed him *Heavy* – who shouldn't have been there at all. He'd been playing craps on board an aircraft carrier, and somehow became involved in a fight. He hit the other guy once, and thought – quite reasonably, given his size – that it was all over. But the other guy managed to pick up a fire-axe, and hit him in the back, giving him a huge gash. He was in hospital for months. But then, when he came out, they sent him to the brig. What had *he* done? *Nothing!* He was the *victim!*

Then, one day, a new prisoner, who'd been put in the same room as Heavy and a lot of other prisoners, claimed he'd been gang-raped during the night. Some of them admitted having anal intercourse with him, but said that he'd been a willing partner, that he'd even suggested it. No formal charges were made, because it could have been embarrassing for us and our officers if it had got out that the Brig hadn't been properly checked that night. Instead, these guys – and Heavy was amongst them – were made to do heavy labour. They were also made to sleep in an absolutely bare room, under bright lights, with no furnishings of any kind, just a bucket for shitting in. And as if that weren't bad enough, *I had to go in every night, every hour on the hour, get these guys on their feet, bring them to attention, dismiss them, and then leave ....*

You had to torment them?

Right ...

This obviously goes deep with you ...

They were all Black guys from the south ... They'd had pretty wretched lives ...

And there you were, making their lives still more wretched. How long did the punishment go on for?

Oh, about a week.

And what effect did it have? On them, I mean ...

They grew steadily more exhausted, steadily more angry ...

And Heavy?

Well, one night, I arrived late, which meant that I had to call them on the half-hour, rather than the hour, and, the next day, someone told them I'd wakened them once too often. That wasn't true – in fact, I'd wakened them one time too few – but they believed it, and when I went in again, I found Heavy looming over me, angry as hell, convinced that I was getting pleasure out of all this ... I wasn't so much scared as sorry, sorry that he could think that.

You feel guilty about what you did as a Brig Guard? That you should have refused to be a party to it?

I should have, but I didn't have the courage. By then it would have meant my going to prison, because I'd lost my religious beliefs.

Like a lot of other people, you were just following orders.

Exactly.

You said earlier that, after the war was over, and you became a student, you joined the Quakers for a while. Was this because of what you'd found yourself willing to do, or not unwilling not to do, while in the Navy?

Sure ... Well ... It's hard to talk about ...

We can move on to other things ...

No – if it isn't hard to talk about, it's probably not *worth* talking about ... While we were still in training, out in California, near San Francisco, a combat instructor took a bunch of us out and gave us a lesson in how, if you're caught without any weapons, you can blind a man with your bare hands, and then ... rip off his face ... I sort of ... I'm sorry ...

You wrote about this in 'After Experience Taught Me ...'

I did.

But it troubles you still ...

I recovered that scene some years later when I was in shallow-level psychotherapy ... It was a strange situation, because the therapist was behind a mirror, and couldn't be seen ... Anyway, we went back to that incident, and I simply broke up, went all over the room ...
 It may be that they didn't really expect us to do that, that they were testing us, to see how willing we were to be stripped of our former attitudes ...

But you didn't think that at the time?

No, no. I believed that's what they expected us to do. I also believed that I had no business being someplace I might have to do such a thing.

Would you have, do you think?

I think I might have ...

Maybe none of us knows what he's capable of, until he sees what he actually does?

But you know, I heard somewhere that in WWII, a very high proportion of the guns 'jammed'.

You mean people couldn't bring themselves to open fire?

Right.

It would be nice to believe that that was true!

Except that I kind of like the fact we didn't lose that war!

Well, you wouldn't have wanted to lose that war because of your better instincts, but maybe there's something to be said for having won it despite them!

Hah!

And the Quakers?

Okay, well, later on, when Korea was starting to hot up, I knew I couldn't go back into the military. I knew I couldn't go to jail either, because by then I was married and had a child to think of. The only alternative was to find support from some religious group, and that's how I ended up going to the Quakers. I'd gone to the Unitarians first, but they were so naïve, always believing the best of people. The Quakers were very different, very courageous, quite prepared to believe the worst about everybody!

When the war did break out, were you called up?

As I recall, I sent in my draft card, telling them I wouldn't be prepared to serve. And they said, 'Look, if things were that bad, we'd ring you up and tell you *all* about it! But for now we don't need people your age, so please:

Go away!'

We've moved rather a long way from The Führer Bunker, *but it's not hard to see how someone who's had the sorts of experiences you've described might be disposed to take an interest in the evil that men do, and to make it a subject of his poetry. In one way or another, the foul rag-and-bone shop of the human heart has always been pretty close to the centre of your concerns.*

That's right.

I'll want to come back to this later, but it seems to me that the urge to conform, the pressure to conform, and the dangers of not resisting the urge and the pressure, are never very far away from your concerns as a writer.

You won't get an argument out of me over that!

I'd like to go back to McClatchy again, if I may. He said he was at a loss to know how to categorise The Führer Bunker. *He didn't want to call it a 'play' because, he said, 'its dramaturgy is too weak, and its details too impacted, for it to hold the stage.' Now, that's a little odd, isn't it? Because, by the time McClatchy wrote that, you'd only ever described* The Führer Bunker *as 'a cycle of poems,' whose individual parts were 'dramatic monologues'?*

Right.

Of course, some years later, you did help to produce a stage version of The Führer Bunker, *but I'm using my words carefully: this was a* stage version *of the poems, not a play. McClatchy seems to be criticizing a hawk for its poor performance as a handsaw.*

I agree with you entirely. Don Hall called it an *opera*, and it clearly had some of the features of an opera, even though it's not for singers. I prefer to think of it as an *oratorio* or *speech cantata*.

How did the stage version come about?

Well, there were a number of stage versions, but the first came about after I ran into Wynn Handman, who ran the American Place Theatre. We'd met years before when I went along to do a review of Lowell's 'The Old Glory', and now he seemed interested in having a play from me. I told him about the *Bunker* poems, and he suggested that I try scripting them for the stage.

When I finally delivered it, my script was given to a German director called Carl Weber. He'd worked with Brecht for many years, so was very experienced. Then a bunch of actors were brought in, two-thirds of them, it's maybe worth saying, Jewish. And over the next several months, the theatre mounted three 'takes', doing it in a totally different way on each occasion. Of these, I thought the second was much the best. The first had been too naturalistic, with the stage setting realistic, each actor taking a single part, the music just like music you would have heard in Berlin during the war years. As a matter of fact, it was the composer of this music – a well-known figure in New York called Richard Peaslee – who suggested that we weren't doing right by the text in staging it this way.

I think it was Peaslee who did the music for Brooks's production of Marat/Sade, *when that was put on in London a few years back.*

Well, in the second 'take', we tried something very different. The stage was open, each part could be played by several actors, the music was very experimental, microphones were buried at several places onstage, speakers were hidden all around the auditorium. If there were several actors onstage at the same time, you might not be sure who was speaking, because the voice coming from downstage right, or wherever, could be coming out of a speaker upstage. Well, we were never able to do the whole of this version, because we ran out of time. But I thought it was great, and so did the friends who saw a run-through.

The third 'take' was much less impressive, which was a pity, because it was the only one seen by the general public. I wasn't around much when rehearsals got started. My private life was in a mess, and I was back teaching again, so I didn't have the time. I assumed they'd carry on from where they left off, because everyone had been so delighted with the second 'take', so I was astonished when I found they'd actually turned their backs on that and gone back to something much more like the first. Each part was played by a single actor again, the music was once again typical of the '40s, the stage sets – they'd built several smaller stages around the auditorium – were once again quite realistic. That would have been bad enough, but at the last moment, they'd brought in a new set-designer, and he'd made a number of weird changes, things I didn't like at all. So, the space between the audience and the stage was filled with junk, particularly wrecked television sets! When I asked what the hell *they* were doing there, I was told that this was a criticism of the German middle class, whose values had made the Hitler period possible. Ridiculous! On top of that, Carl had decided to place several cages of rabbits on the stage! Again, I had no idea what *they* were doing there. There *is* a place in the text where the Goebbels children are called 'poor trapped rabbits', but that didn't seem to be behind it, and when I asked, he said, 'Well they might have had things like that for meat.' Well, yes, they *might* have!

If they'd wanted verisimilitude, crates of champagne would have made more sense than cages of rabbits.

Right! I protested, but they went ahead anyway. I don't know what other action I might have taken, but I decided to put my trust in their greater theatrical experience and waited to see what would happen. What happened was that, since it looked like a play, most of the reviewers complained – like McClatchy – that it wasn't much of a play. Of course, it wasn't meant to be *any*. But if you stage it so that people expect one, they'll be disappointed.

The one exception among reviewers was Clive Barnes, who wrote a very intelligent, very favourable review. The trouble is that he'd been reviewer for *The New York Times* until two weeks before, and now he was writing for *The New York Post*. Our sense of timing again! If he'd still been at the *Times*, we might be running yet!

Another quite different staging was done at Ypsilanti, Michigan. For this, the director, Annette Martin, and I did a new script – largely her work – which was much better. The staging was altogether unrealistic. At centre stage was a 20' bust of Hitler, carved out of Styrofoam, and there were ramps, stairways and landings all around, where the chorus could march, hold processions, and so on. The poems were broken apart and scrambled into one another, and, once again, a rôle could be taken by two or three actors, which made it easier to dramatize the conflict inside individuals. Sadly, the actors – unlike the splendid New York cast – were amateurs. Some had never been on stage before. Still, it was, on the whole, a much more successful mounting of the piece. But no-one from New York – no-one influential, that is – saw it.

The Führer Bunker *was obviously a time-consuming project, but not so time-consuming that you weren't able to work on other things besides. In 1979, for example, you published* If Birds Build with Your Hair, *a collection that proved quite reassuring for at least one of the admirers who'd not been able to follow you down the Reich Chancellery steps ...*

Oh?

Contrasting it with what he called the 'macabre romp with Adolph and Eva', Dana Gioia declared: 'I am happy to say that this new collection shows Snodgrass at his best again – witty, wise and endlessly inventive.'

Ah.

He did rather spoil things by going on to describe the poems, without qualification, as contemporary pastorals, *which suggested that their apparent subjects – the birds' nest, the orchard, the barn, and so on – were their real subjects as well, when in fact their real subjects were, manifestly, human concerns of one kind or another ... It's tempting to say that your reviewer couldn't see the mood for the trees. – Or perhaps talking of apparent and real subjects is misleading. Because a poem like 'Owls' isn't only* apparently *about a great horned owl and its mate and* really *about you and your wife – it's about both. What I should have said was that Gioia's description of the poems was inadequate because it suggested that there was nothing more to them than could be found on the surface.*

But let's leave that issue on one side, because I'd like, if I may, to ask you about the prosody of 'Owls', which I gather derives from the call of the bird ...

That's right. The rhythm of the first line -

> Wait; the great horned owls

- is based on the rhythm of their call, which sounds like this:

> HOO, hoo HOO, HOO, HOO

And the lines which follow play variations on that. The second adds a handful of unaccented syllables:

> Calling from the wood's edge, listen

And after the third line, which goes back to the basic pattern -

> There: the dark male, low

– the fourth adds yet more light syllables:

> And booming, tremoring the whole valley

I take it this sprang from your interest in Whitman? Only you'd already demonstrated a liking for his use of rhythmic themes and variations, in your poem about Van Gogh's 'The Starry Night'.

Yes, but there I'd not taken a rhythm as my theme, I'd taken a pattern of vowel sounds. It was only later that I decided to try a rhythm, maybe because the rhythm in question was so different from any of Whitman's. I didn't want to appear too derivative.

You were happily married at this time, but it would seem that not everything in your personal life was going so well. 'Cherry Saplings' and 'Setting Out' both suggest that you were having serious difficulties elsewhere. Am I right in thinking that both of these have to do with your son, the son you'd had by your previous wife?

Yes. And the gulf that had opened up between us, or been created between us.

And 'Coming Down from the Acropolis' and 'The Sealchie's Son'? They weren't included in If Birds Build with Your Hair, *but they were written in the same period.*

They're about him too. My third wife and I had taken him on a trip to Europe. His mother obviously didn't want him to go, and after we'd arrived in Europe he began to get letters from her, letters which put him in a blue funk. Finally, while we were in Athens, he announced he was going home.

As described in the closing lines of 'Coming Down from the Acropolis'?

Right. – As for 'The Sealchie's Son', that's based on one of the old ballads collected by Childs, a wonderful song called 'The Great Sealchie of Sule Skerry'. It was actually recorded by Joan Baez, but you'd never know how wonderful it was from her rendition, because, typically, she fucks it up in the second stanza, doesn't understand what she's singing.

A sealchie is what, exactly?

It's a mythical creature, half-seal, half-man, half-god. There are too many *halves* there, but you get the idea. In the ocean, it looks like a seal, but when it wants to it can come onto the land, where it takes on the appearance of a human. Anyway, in the ballad, the sealchie goes to claim his son:

> It shall come to pass on a summer's day
> When the sun shines hot on every stone
> That I shall take my little young son
> And teach him how to swim the foam.

'The Sealchie's Son' was about my hopes of casting a spell to bring Russ back to Camille and me, here in Erieville.

As to the first two poems you mentioned, the ones which appeared in *If Birds Build with Your Hair*: 'Setting Out' is about Russ's turning away from us and the rather settled life we had here in the woods, and 'Cherry Saplings' is about how some people are content to damage the best things you can plant.

Some years later, but again while still working on The Führer Bunker, *you published* A Locked House, *which won high praise from another of the work-in-progress's detractors, J.D. McClatchy. He said the book contained poems which 'would be reckoned among [your] finest work'. It's a surprising volume in some ways, with a number of poems whose style and tone hark back to the ones that first gained you public attention, in* Heart's Needle.

My marriage to Camille had broken up, and I was as crushed by this as I had earlier been by the loss – what I had *thought* was the loss – of Cynthia, my daughter. So if *A Locked House* goes back to *Heart's Needle* in its style and mood – and I agree that it does – that's the likely explanation.

You'd been writing a lot of free verse, and now you were back to using metre again. Was this connected in any way?

I had always written free verse, but as a younger man I used to throw most of it away. Later on, it was the metrical verse I was throwing away, and the free verse I was keeping. Probably because of all my work on early music, I'd got to the point where I felt I could produce a satisfying music without formal metrics. But then, after the breakdown of my marriage, I found I couldn't produce the sort of poem I wanted without the stiffening given by a stricter form. Without that, I felt I was going to produce poems that were sloppy and sentimental.

All seven of the poems in A Locked House *were about that breakdown, and the shock, anger, bafflement, and sadness that it involved. But when you brought out your* Selected Poems *in 1987, you added an eighth poem to the other seven, one which was totally different in character ...*

'D.D. Byrde Callyng Jennie Wrenn', yes.

Can you say something about that?

Well, after Camille left, I was leading a very unpleasant life. People I'd thought were friends turned on me. I got involved with a number of younger women, women who, though they'd initiate the thing, were terrified of any kind of commitment. They were the kind of women who'd screw you just so they didn't have to hold hands!

Hah! These were women of the kind you describe in 'A Teenager' – '...spoiled, groomed, fairy-story rich'?

Actually no. 'A Teenager' is about something that happened while I was still married, possibly to my second wife Janice, and went off on a week's engagement at Lake Forest College in Illinois. I also gave a reading at an arts high school nearby which sent two young girls over to pick me up in the one girl's Volkswagen Beetle. I felt that the sex talk between them was really pointed at me, and thought about trying to hustle the redhead, who *was* gorgeous. But the act reported by the poem quelled such notions, and when I thought it over, she seemed so artificial that I was glad I'd resisted.

How long did this unpleasant life of yours continue?

About four or five years, I guess, and I really was miserable much of that time. I wanted an enduring relationship, and didn't seem able to find it.

And then?

Then Kathy came into my life.

And it's your relationship with her that's being celebrated in 'D.D. Byrde Callyng Jennie Wrenn'?

That's right.

The poem is a persuasion, like Marlowe's 'The Passionate Shepherd to His Love' or Herrick's 'To the Virgins, to Make Much of Time'. But it's a persuasion with a difference, because its form is that of a nursery rhyme – a particularly witty and inventive nursery rhyme. – I take it the poem was written after you'd begun collaborating with DeLoss McGraw, since, as I understand it, it was he who first got you interested in the nursery-rhyme about Cock Robin in which Jenny Wren figures.

I'm not certain – I'm very bad about dating things. I believe Kathy and I were already living together when I first heard from him. The versions of 'Cock Robin' I knew best didn't usually involve Jenny Wren. It might be that she comes partly from Ralph Hodgson's 'Eve', which I once heard Dylan Thomas read, and which goes something like this:

> Oh what a clatter
> When titmouse and Jenny Wren
>   Saw him successful and taking his leave.
> How the birds rated him,
> How they all hated him,
>   How they all pitied poor, motherless Eve!

The collaboration with McGraw proved to be remarkably fruitful, leading to the publication, first of limited fine press editions like A Colored Poem *and* The House the Poet Built, *and then of the books,* The Death of Cock Robin *and* W.D.'s Midnight Carnival. *How did it get started?*

It got started after Del wrote to me in the early '80s, saying that he was working on a couple of pictures – coloured lithographs – inspired by poems in *Heart's Needle* and *After Experience,* and asking if he could use my name in the titles. Later on, he sent copies of the lithographs. He'd called one of them, 'W.D. Snodgrass, You Sentimental Fool', and the other, 'W.D. Snodgrass, Silly Man, Come Out of the Storm'. I wrote and told him how much we liked them. And I wasn't exaggerating.

After that, he did a whole series of paintings based on my work, and showed them at a gallery in Los Angeles. Kathy and I were getting ready to leave for Mexico when we received a bunch of slides he'd taken of the paintings in that exhibition. We were too busy to give them more than a glance, but after we arrived in Mexico we gave them a closer look, and I was immediately captivated. One in particular caught my eye: 'W.D. Attempts to Save Cock Robin'. That's the one with W.D. carrying Cock Robin away on his back – a really beautiful painting. But there were a couple of others that had to do with Cock Robin, and they were very striking too.

And then?

Well, I'd gone to Mexico intending to carry on with *The Führer Bunker*, but suddenly found myself writing about these paintings instead. I hadn't tried anything like that since I was about eighteen or nineteen, but after so much time working on serious topics, it was a great pleasure to do something that wasn't so serious, at least on the surface. The poems came very swiftly too, which was kind of nice.

So The Führer Bunker *was put on hold?*

Temporarily, yes. But it was around this time I began to feel I *could* finish the cycle. Up till then, I'd never been sure, and the doubts had been especially bad when I'd been living alone. Now, though, I began to think, *I can finish this.* You know, after Rilke finished the *Duino Elegies,* he thought, *There, my career is over – I can die tomorrow.* But then, within a matter of weeks, he'd produced over a hundred sonnets, poems totally unlike the *Elegies* – playful and light ... I once wrote an introduction to some of those poems, in which I said that they weren't *necessary* works. The *Elegies* had been *necessary,* but these later poems were a kind of bonus, an overflow. Now, I'm not trying to put myself in Rilke's league, but there was a similar change between *The Führer Bunker* and these poems.

Earlier on, I suggested that conformism has never been very far away from your concerns as a writer. Individual poems are devoted to it in your first two collections, but thereafter it becomes the leitmotif of whole volumes. Remains *deals with it in a family setting,* The Führer Bunker *deals with it in a military and political setting ...*

I suppose so.

And if they approach it in a different way – most obviously, by employing allegory – The Death of Cock Robin and W.D.'s Midnight Carnival are also given over to the same phenomenon. Thus, in the earlier cycle, the charges against Cock Robin come down to his being out-of-step: 'he sings beyond other birds' range; his tunes baffle and defeat us; he dresses in a fashion/Neither generic nor respectable,' etc., etc. And in the later cycle, the Wire Walker maintains a precarious balance knowing that the earthbound audience is just praying for him to come a cropper: 'Are such heights moral?/ Let's check his feet for the pure slime/ We live in: some deep flaw or crime/ Drives any anti-social climb.'

Yes, I'll go along with that.

But would I be right in thinking that more recent events in your life were giving this old concern an added vitality? I mean, it's hard to read a poem like 'The Charges Against Cock Robin' without being reminded of the charges levelled at you after the publication of The Führer Bunker.

I was certainly thinking about the terrible things that were being said about me: the claim that I was pro-Nazi, that I was anti-Semitic, and so on.

And a poem like 'W.D. Is Concerned about the Character Assassination of Cock Robin' is just as hard to read without being put in mind of the difficulties you experienced at the hands of former friends after your break-up with Camille?

These things surely played a part.

Would you be happy to have the poems you wrote while collaborating with McGraw described as 'light verse'? The term is very vague, I know, but if it's used in some such way as Armour used it, to describe verse that's written in a spirit of play, even verse that has a serious underlying purpose, would you be happy with it? Because, of course, The Death of Cock Robin *and* W.D.'s Midnight Carnival, *are playful in manner – as Philip Raisor says, the poems seem intended to cock a snook at Addison, who damned acrostics, anagrams, patterns and various other devices as instances of false wit – yet they deal with matters that are deadly serious.*

I guess I'm not fond of the term 'light'. I remember, Oscar Williams put Auden's 'Refugee Blues' in a section of so-called 'light verse' and we were all horrified. My poems probably wish to belong to whatever category fits a piece like that one. But, after all, it's not a poet's privilege to classify his work. *You* get to do that. As the politicians say, *Call me anything you like, but spell my name right!*

Your relationship with McGraw has proved to be very fruitful. Apart from the poems we've just been talking about, you've produced The Kinder Capers *and* To Shape a Song, *both published as fine press editions. Do you expect to work with him again?*

I doubt that we'll do more collaborating. But I've thought that several times before ...

Before becoming a writer, you trained for a career as a musician. You gave that up when you realized that you didn't have the technique, or the dedication, but music has always been a great passion of yours. Did you ever collaborate with a composer?

No, I never did. Some of the poems in *Heart's Needle* were once set to music, by Michael Torke.

Oh?

You know him?

I only know one of his pieces – The Yellow Pages *– but he's a well-known figure in contemporary music.*

Well, he gave them big Mahleresque settings, which seemed not to fit. I was pleased that someone was interested in setting the poems, but I've always felt that there's no point in setting a poem unless you markedly change it, and this didn't seem like the right change.

Isn't that a little strange, given the influence on Heart's Needle *of Mahler's music?*

But the music which influenced *Heart's Needle* was the music of *Kindertotenlieder*, and these settings were like the heavy stuff – *Das Lied von der Erde*, and so on.

I can't think of many composers who've had real success with contemporary poetry. Boulez's settings of Char and Mallarmé are interesting, as are Birtwhistle's settings of Celan.

I'm afraid I don't know them.

Elliott Carter did very well by Frost, but to my ear rather less well by Lowell and Bishop. The best things I've heard in a long time are by another English composer, George Benjamin. He's done an astonishingly good setting of Stevens's 'The Snow Man' – you have to be well wrapped-up to listen to it – and an equally marvellous setting of Yeats's 'Long-Legged Fly'.

I'll have to look out for them. I'm afraid I don't listen to much contemporary music. A piece I do admire enormously is Luciano Berio's *Sinfonia*. At one point, you hear a version of the scherzo from Mahler's 5th and, simultaneously, several voices, speaking in different languages, about completely divergent topics, and doing so at various tempos. It should sound chaotic, but it doesn't: it's quite incredible.

Your most recent collection – I'm excluding The Führer Bunker *– is* Each in His Season, *and I'd like to ask about some of the poems in this remarkably heterogeneous book, beginning with a serious one, and then moving on to a more light-hearted one.*

Go ahead.

The serious one is 'Elena Ceausescu's Bed'. If The Führer Bunker *is meant as a challenge to the idea that the tyrants of this world have nothing in common with us, this poem seems meant as a challenge to the idea that we are unstained by their crimes – that is, we democrats, we church-goers, we believers in kindness and consideration:*

> *How many had been driven*
> *Homeless and hungering while I had my own*
> *Bed, my own room? How many had been given*
>
> *Lives at hard labour while our markets rose*
> *And we had all we asked for in the lands*
> *Of milk and honey? ...*

The poem seems quite closely related to 'Coming Down from the Acropolis', insofar as both concern themselves with what I'll loosely describe as civilization's debts to barbarism.

Yes.

Why Elena Ceausescu's bed, I wonder?

Well, Kathy and I went to a translators' conference in Romania, but arrived later than most of the other people. They had been taken out to a castle in the countryside, but because of our late arrival we were taken to a place off the highway going into Bucharest. One of the first things to strike us was the bed, which was absolutely enormous, and, like all of the *permanent* furnishings, beautifully carved. (I used to like to carve, and really appreciated that kind of thing.) Anyway, we were told a little later that that house, with its bed, had belonged to Elena Ceausescu.

How long after the régime's downfall was this?

Oh, not long – a year or two, I guess. It was kind of strange, knowing that she'd slept in that bed.

The more light-hearted poem I wanted to ask you about is 'A Curse', which, whenever I read it, has me laughing out loud. It makes me want to say of you what Balak was supposed to have said of Balaam: 'He whom you bless is blessed, and he whom you curse is cursed'!

Hah!

What's the story behind that poem?

We were going to Mexico one year, and we wanted to take a harpsichord for Kathy to play. We knew of an instrument-maker in town, so we went and talked to this guy, explaining what we wanted, and telling him when we had to have it by. He said he could do it, so we gave him all the things I mention in the poem – the applewood, the ivory and so on – and waited for the thing to be delivered. But it never was. Every time we got in touch, he'd give us an excuse – one excuse after another …

You never did take delivery of the instrument?

No. – I guess we should have known better. My daughter had been acquainted with the guy, and she'd warned us that he wasn't trustworthy, but ...

And the address? Against A.H., who does not make instruments. Are A.H. the man's real initials?

No, I showed the original version to a lawyer, who said, 'Go right ahead and publish – if you've got $20,000 you don't need'!

Whew! So, why those initials? You weren't comparing this man to Hitler, I take it?

Adolf Hitler, Ass Hole ...

Hah!

I have a lot of fun reading that poem.

Another very light-hearted poem, which, like 'A Curse', has its source in something other people might have felt didn't have a funny side, is 'An Envoi, Post-TURP'. Here you joke about one of the consequences of having had surgical treatment for prostatitis ...

Trans-Urethral Resectioning of the Prostate, or TURP, for short.

The operation was a success, I gather?

Oh sure. But that poem's about a side effect of the operation that nobody bothered to inform us of in advance ...

Retrograde ejaculation.

Right. As you might imagine, it was all a bit puzzling at first.

I'm sure it was!

Later on, we discovered that it's quite common amongst people who've undergone the treatment. It's not in the least bit painful, but unless you know what's going on, it *is* very puzzling!

I'd like to ask you about the volume's title sequence, 'Each in His Season', which is divided into four sections: 'Spring Suite', 'Summer Sequence', 'Autumn Variations' and 'Snow Songs'. Does the sequence owe anything to the four sonnets – the sonneti dimostrativi, *as they were known – which accompanied Vivaldi's famous work,* The Four Seasons, *and which you yourself translated back in the early '80s?*

It may owe something to them, but I'm not conscious of it. Do you think there's a debt?

Well, yes and no. Fred Chappell wrote a very interesting essay about this sequence, which begins with his saying that, when he first read it, he suspected that it was closely modelled on The Four Seasons. *He later saw fit to change his opinion, but how he could have entertained it isn't clear to me. I mean, Vivaldi's piece offers a fairly traditional picture of the seasons, and of life more generally. It has its bleaker details, of course – as when the storms play havoc with the crops, and the animal being pursued by huntsmen is brought to its knees, terrified – but these only serve to emphasize the positive character of the picture, taken as a whole. By contrast, the attractive details of the picture you offer in 'Each in His Season' only serve to emphasize its generally negative character. Even something as normally charged with positive associations as the appearance in spring of green shoots takes on, in 'Each in His Season', a quite negative charge:*

> Then, out of the black soil, green shoots
> Up – as if fleeing its own roots
> Or something else it must have found
> Terrifying in the ground ...

So, your debt to Vivaldi, if there is one, isn't borne out of your having modelled the sequence on his piece, but on your having written something which is its negation. The world of this sequence is a pretty comfortless one, wouldn't you say?

Well, one of us said something earlier about civilization's debt to barbarism ...

Let me ask you another question about 'Each in His Season'. Chappell sees it as an attempt on your part to exploit, to a still greater extent than in your previous work, the musical properties of language ...

That surely is true.

But what did you make of his claim that, throughout the sequence, you're trying to create verbal analogues for musical devices, that, with a particular slant rhyme, say, you were trying to create something analogous to a musical dissonance, or that, with a certain compound word, you were trying to create an analogue for a tone cluster, and so on?

If I was, I wasn't conscious of it.

But would you accept the claims he makes, about these things being analogous in their effects?

I would accept his overall notion, but many of the specific examples seem pushed pretty far. Still, I'm really pleased to have Fred consider anything of mine, agree or not.

I know you play a lot of music, and listen to a great deal more. Are there any direct ways, would you say, in which your poetry has been affected by your love of music.

Oh, certainly.

Can you give an example?

Well, what you might call the *discordancy* of some of my poems is probably due to my having learnt to admire some of the great compositions of the twentieth century – Berg's two operas, *Wozzeck* and *Lulu*, Bartok's *The Miraculous Mandarin*, and his six string quartets, that piece by Berio I mentioned earlier, *Sinfonia* … I wrote somewhere that *I gave up music, it never gave me up*. It influences me in all sorts of ways, most of which I'm sure I can't even guess at.

You're seventy-one this year, and still going strong. As I understand it, you're putting the finishing touches to not just one, nor just two, but three different books.

That's right. There's the *Selected Translations*, which is giving me all sorts of trouble at the moment.

Oh?

Well, I've sent many papers to the archives and many books to dealers, with the result that I'm having to call people and ask them to check titles in the original languages, and other things like that. It's all very frustrating.

And the other two books?

I'm just about to finish a book of autobiographical sketches, which I'm calling *After-Images*. There's one more chapter to write, about visiting my home town for a fiftieth high school reunion. I have to go back and get a clearer picture of that place. It's a small industrial city which, since the death of the steel industry here, has collapsed shockingly.

The third book is a collection of critical essays, which I've decided to call *To Sound Like Yourself,* which is a phrase from Miles Davis.

It sounds like a phrase Berryman once used, in the essay about his own development that's included in The Freedom of the Poet.

I don't think I've seen that, but you remind me of something he said in his poetry workshop, which was that a poet first has to find his own voice, then has to find the opposite voice, and then has to synthesize them.

Anyway, *To Sound Like Yourself* is short of one chapter too, an essay about conventional metrics. I've been working on it for a while now, and hope it won't resist for too much longer.

And publication?

The translations should come out next year, but I kind of doubt I'll get either of the other books out before '99. I'm too fucking picky: everything always takes three times as long as I predict.

What was it Dr Johnson said? 'What is written without effort is in general read without pleasure.'

≡

Bibliography

(Compiled by Kathleen Snodgrass)

Primary Works

Poetry

Books

Heart's Needle, Knopf, New York, 1959; reprinted 1983; Marvell, Yorkshire, 1960.
After Experience, Harper, New York, 1968; Oxford University Press, London, 1968.
The Führer Bunker: A Cycle of Poems in Progress, BOA Editions, Brockport, New York, 1977.
Remains: A Sequence of Poems, BOA Editions, Brockport, New York, 1985.
Selected Poems: 1957-1987, Soho, New York, 1987.
W. D.'s Midnight Carnival, with DeLoss McGraw, Artra, Encinitas, 1988.
The Death of Cock Robin, with DeLoss McGraw, University of Delaware Press, Newark, 1989.
Each In His Season, BOA Editions, Brockport, New York, 1993.
The Fuehrer Bunker: The Complete Cycle, BOA Editions, Brockport, New York, 1995.

Limited Fine Press Editions

Remains: Poems, S.S. Gardons, (pseudonym), Perishable Press, Mt. Horeb, WI, 1970.
If Birds Build with Your Hair, Nadja, New York, 1979.
These Trees Stand, portrait series by Robert Mahon, Carol Joyce, New York, 1981.
Heinrich Himmler: Platoons and Files, Pterodactyl, Cumberland, IA, 1982.
Magda Goebbels, Palaemon, Winston-Salem, NC, 1983.
The Boy Made of Meat, wood engravings by Gillian Tyler, W B. Ewert, Concord, NH, 1983.
D. D. Byrde Calling Jennie Wrenn, W. B. Ewert, Concord, NH, 1984.
A Locked House, W. B. Ewert, Concord, NH, 1986.
A Colored Poem, colour lithographs by DeLoss McGraw, Brighton, San Diego, 1986.
The House the Poet Built, colour lithographs by DeLoss McGraw, Brighton, San Diego, 1986.
The Kinder Capers, illustrations by DeLoss McGraw, Nadja, New York, 1986.
The Midnight Carnival, original etchings by DeLoss McGraw, Brighton, San Diego, 1988.
To Shape a Song, illustrations by DeLoss McGraw, Nadja, New York, 1988.
Autumn Variations, Nadja, New York, 1990.
Snow Songs, Nadja, New York, 1992.
Spring Cycle, Nadja, NewYork, 1994.

Pamphlets

Spaulding Distinguished Lectures, University of New Hampshire Press, Durham, 1969.

Lullaby: The Comforting of Cock Robin, Nadja, New York, 1988.

Broadsides and Posters

'After Experience Taught Me . .', *Ligature* 68, Madison Park, Chicago, 1968.
'Coming Down from the Acropolis', The Rook Society, Derry, PA, 1976.
'Mutability', *Northern Lights*, Palaemon, Winston-Salem, NC, 1983.
'Owls', graphics by Marta Anderson, W.B. Ewert, Concord, NH, 1983.
'Magda Goebbels: 12 April 1945', Palaemon, Winston-Salem, NC, 1984.
'Old Jewelry', *Fifty Years of American Poetry*, Palaemon, Winston-Salem, NC, 1984.
'The Death of Cock Robin: Poems and Paintings', with DeLoss McGraw, University Art Museum, California State University, Long Beach, 1986.
'Lullaby: The Comforting of Cock Robin', hand-coloured etching by DeLoss McGraw, Brighton, San Diego, 1987.
'Three Versicles', W.B. Ewert, Concord, NH, 1987.
'Dance Suite: Minuet in F##', W.B. Ewert, Concord, NH, 1989.
'Dance Suite: Mexican Hat Dance', W.B. Ewert, Concord, NH, 1990.
'He Bare Him Up, He Bare Him Down …', W.B. Ewert, Concord, NH, 1991.
'Winter', W.B. Ewert, Concord, NH, 1995.
'The Noxious 25¢ Song', W.B. Ewert, Concord, NH, 1996.

Uncollected

'"The Last Toot" from *Whatever Happened to Father?*' *Experiment: A Quarterly of New Poetry* 6, 1951, 9.
'Good Friday', *Western Review* 15, Summer 1951, 260; reprinted in *Poems from the Iowa Poetry Workshop*, foreword by Paul Engle, Prairie, Iowa City, 1951.
'A Character', *New Mexico Quarterly* 28, 1956.
'Letter', *Transatlantic Review*, Summer 1956.
'Critic', *The Formalist* 3, no. 2, 1992, 29.
'Nocturnes', 'Lifelong' and 'A Presence', *Agenda* 34, no. 1, 1996, 5-13.

Translations

Books

Gallows Songs, by Christian Morgenstern, trans. with Lore Segal, University of Michigan Press, Ann Arbor, 1967.
Five Folk Ballads (*Cinci balade populare*), Cartea Romaneasca, Bucharest, 1993.

Limited Fine Press Editions

Six Troubadour Songs, Burning Deck, Providence, RI, 1977.
Traditional Hungarian Songs, Charles Seluzicki, Baltimore, 1978.
Six Minnesinger Songs, Burning Deck, Providence, RI, 1983.
Antonio Vivaldi, The Four Seasons, Targ, New York, 1984.

Star and Other Poems, by Mihai Eminescu, W.B. Ewert, Concord, NH, 1990.

Broadsides and Posters

'Star', by Mihai Eminescu, Charles Seluzicki, Baltimore, 1982.
'Somnoroasa Pasarele' ('Now the Songbirds, All Adrowse'), by Mihai Eminescu, trans. with Augustin Maissen, W.B. Ewert, Concord, NH, 1985.

Uncollected

'The Mother', trans. with Tanya Tolstoy from the pseudonymous Russian, Kozma Petrovich Prutkov, *The Hudson Review* 11, no. 3, August 1958, 368-369.
'In Praise of Reason', trans. of 'Lob des Hohen Verstands' from Gustav Mahler's *Des Knaben Wunderhorn*, *Quarterly Review of Literature* 10, 1960, 140-141.
'Servant Girl's Dream', by Christian Morgenstern, trans. with Lore Groszmann (Segal), *Poetry* 98, September 1961, 365.
'The Lady and the Tarantula: A Fable', trans. with Tanya Tolstoy from the pseudonymous Russian, Kozma Petrovich Prutkov, *Tri-Quarterly* 1, Fall 1963, 33.
'Love of Honour', The Heron and the Racing Rig', 'Romanza', 'A Poet's Will', 'Remembrance of Things Past', 'Junker Schmidt', 'The Worm and the Deaconess', 'Forget-Me-Nots and Footboards', 'My Portrait', trans. with Tanya Tolstoy from the pseudonymous Russian, Kozma Petrovich Prutkov, *Poetry* 104, July 1964, 203-209.
'Poems in the Style of Heine', trans. with Tanya Tolstoy from the pseudonymous Russian, Kozma Petrovich Prutkov, *North American Review* 1, Summer 1964, 49.
'Autumn', trans. with Tanya Tolstoy, from the pseudonymous Russian, Kozma Petrovich Prutkov, *Tri-Quarterly* 1, Fall 1964, 33.
'Junker Schmidt', trans. with Tanya Tolstoy from the pseudonymous Russian, Kozma Petrovich Prutkov, *Eight Lines and Under*, ed. William Cole, Macmillan, New York, 1967, 101.
'You, the Heaven's Domed Height', by Balint Balassi, *The New Hungarian Quarterly* 11, Summer 1970, 65.
'Miorita' (Ewe Lamb), Romanian ballad, trans. with Simone Draghici and Ioan Popa, *Miorita*, Editura Albatros, Bucharest, Romania, 1972; reprinted in *Agenda* 12, Autumn 1974, 64-67, and in *Romanian Folk Arts*, Romanian Library, n.d., New York.
'The Merry Cemetery at Sapinta', *Romanian Bulletin*, January 1974, 49-53.
'Mass for the Dead' and 'White Doe', *Counter/Measures* 3, 1974.
'Mesterul Manole' ('Master-Builder Manole'), Romanian ballad, *Romanian Bulletin* 5, September 1976, 6-8; reprinted in *Tribuna Romaniei* 5, 1 October 1976.
'Dalea-Damean and Sila', Romanian ballad, *Romanian Bulletin*, 6 June 1977; reprinted in *Miorita* 5, January 1978, 88-91, and in *Oxford Quarterly Review*, 1, nos. 2-3, Summer/Autumn 1996.
'Four Spanish Songs' ('Toda Mi Vida Hos Ame', by Milan, 'Si Me Llaman', by Mudarra, 'Cucu, Cucu', by Del Encina, 'Dale Si Le Das', Anon), *Punto de Contacto / Point of Contact*, 1, no. 4, July 1977.
'Soarele si Luna' ('The Sun and the Moon'), Romanian ballad, *Romanian Bulletin* 6, October 1977, 6-7.
'Six Romanian Folk Songs', *Odyssey* 2, November 1977, 9-10.
'La Roussee Du Joly Mois De May', by Jehan Plancon, trans. with Michael Valentin, 'Cesses

Mortels', by Pierre Guedron, trans. with Leigh Banks, 'Qui Veut Chasser Une Migraine', by Gabriel Bataille, *Negative Capability* 5, no. 1, Winter 1985, 69-82.
'If Boughs Tap …' and 'From the Night', by Mihai Eminescu, trans. with Nicolae Babuts, *Tribuna Romaniei*, Bucharest, Romania, 16.340, 15 May 1987, 10.
'Dog After Love', by Yehuda Amichai, *Grand Street*, Fall 1989.
'Epitaphs from Sapinta', twenty epitaphs from grave markers in a Romanian cemetery, *Romanian Folk Arts*, Romanian Library, n.d., New York.
'Creation', 'Solemnly', 'Thieves', 'I bound Up the Trees' Eyes', by Marin Sorescu, *Poetry* CLIX, no. 4, 1992, 191-4.
'These Spare and Splendid Words I Sing', by Arnaut Daniel, *The Formalist* 4, no. 2, 1993, 67-69.
'An Evening with the Author' and 'Watchman', by Leszek Szaruga, trans. by W.D. and K.B. Snodgrass with Peter Lengyel and Justyna Kostkowska; 'Frames', 'Fortress', 'The Convicted', by Marin Sorescu, trans. with Dona Rosu and Luciana Costea, *Salmagundi* 97, Winter 1993, 110-111.
'Then Daylight Came' ('Owe, Sol Aber Mir'), by Heinrich von Morungen, 'These Spare and Splendid Words I Sing' ('Chanson do'ill mot so plan e prim') by Arnaut Daniel, 'The Organ Grinder' ('Der Leiermann' from *Die Winterreise*), by Johann Müller and Franz Schubert, *The Formalist* 4, no. 1, 1993, 33.
'Atavism' and 'This', by Marin Sorescu, trans. with K.B. Snodgrass and Justyna Kostkowska, *The Southern California Anthology* 11, 1994, 56-57.
'Informing on a Couple Unknown Guys', by Leszek Szaruga, trans. with K.B. Snodgrass and Justyna Kostkowska, *Columbia* 24/25, 1995, 23.
'Between', 'Correctional Colony' and 'Licentia Poetica', by Leszek Szaruga, trans. with K.B. Snodgrass and Justyna Kostkowska, *The Review* 1, Autumn 1995.
'Dialogue', 'Co-Dependency', '[Let's Put This in Brackets]', by Leszek Szaruga, trans. with K.B. Snodgrass and Jusyna Kostkowska; 'Toma Alimos', Romanian ballad, 'Dallea-Damean and Sila', Romanian ballad, 'Behind Closed Doors', 'Frames', 'Transcendental', 'Peasants', 'Troy', 'An Amoeba', by Marin Sorescu, trans. with Dona Rosu and Luciana Costea, *Oxford Quarterly Review* 1, nos. 2-3, Summer/Autumn 1996, 56-79.
'Toma Alimos', Romanian ballad, trans. with Nicolae Babuts and Sever Trifu, *Romanian Bulletin* 8, no. 1, 6-7; reprinted in *Oxford Quarterly Review* 1, nos. 2-3, Summer/Autumn 1996, 56-79.
'La Steaua' by Mihai Eminescu, trans. with Sever Trifu and Neli Ament, *Romanian Bulletin* 8, no. 1, 6-7.
'Pois Preyatz Me, Senhor', 'Can Par la Flor', 'Be Man Perdut', by Bernart de Ventadorn, Jacket Notes, *The Testament of Tristan*, Martin Best, Hyperion Records, CD-A66211.

Criticism

Books

In Radical Pursuit, Harper, New York, 1975.

Uncollected Reviews

'Elegance in Marianne Moore', *Western Review* 19, no. 3, Autumn 1954, 57-64.
'Voice as Visions', Review of *Man Now*, by William Burford; *The Dancing Bears*, by W.S.

Merwin; *The Death Bell*, by Vernon Watkins, *Western Review* 19, no. 3, Spring 1995.
'Nobodies of Prominence', Review of *Greta Garbo*, by John Bainbridge; *Lawrence of Arabia: A Biographical Enquiry*, by Richard Aldington; *The Mint* by T.E. Lawrence, *Western Review* 20, Spring 1956, 231-239.
'Spring Verse Chronicle', Review of *Words for the Wind*, by Theodore Roethke, *Paterson, Five*, by William Carlos Williams, *95 Poems*, by E E. Cummings, *The Magic Maker: E.E. Cumm-ings*, by Charles Norman, *Goodbye Earth and Other Poems*, by I.A. Richards, *The Hudson Review* 12, Spring 1959, 114-123; partially reprinted in *William Carlos Williams: The Critical Heritage*, ed. Charles Doyle, Routledge, London and Boston, 1980.
'Four Gentlemen; Two Ladies', Review of *Thrones: 96-109 de los Cantares*, by Ezra Pound, *The Self-Made Man*, by Reed Whittemore, *Selected Poems* by Robert Duncan, *Scrimshaw*, by Winfield Townley Scott, *A Water Walk by Villa d'Este*, by Jean Garrigue, *Valentines to the Wide World*, by Mona Van Duyn, *The Hudson Review* 13, Spring 1960, 120-131.
'Gottfried Benn', Review of *Primal Vision: Selected Writings of Gottfried Benn*, ed. Ernst Basch, *The Hudson Review* 14, Spring 1961, 118-126.
Review of *The Patterns of Hardy's Poetry*, by Samuel Hynes, *College English* 23, January 1962, 322-23.
'The Last Poems of Theodore Roethke', Review of *The Far Field* and *Sequence, Sometime Metaphysical*, *The New York Review of Books* 3, no. 4, 8 October 1964.
'In Praise of Robert Lowell', Review of *The Old Glory*, *The New York Review of Books* 3, no. 8, 3 December 1964, 8, 10.

Uncollected Essays

'Play Shows Struggle', letter to editor on *Mister Roberts*, *Daily Iowan*, 27 May 1955.
Foreword to *Syracuse Poems*, Syracuse University, Dept., of English, Syracuse, NY, 1969.
Foreword to *Syracuse Poems*, Syracuse University, Dept., of English, Syracuse, NY, 1972.
'Poetry since Yeats: An Exchange of Views', symposium with Stephen Spender, Patrick Kavanagh, and Thomas Kinsella, *Tri-Quarterly* 4, 1975, 100-106.
Foreword to *Syracuse Poems*, Syracuse University, Dept., of English, Syracuse, NY, 1976.
Foreword to *For They Are My Friends*, by Tom Marotta, Art Reflections, New York, 1977.
Preface to *Cedarhome*, by Barton Sutter, BOA Editions, Brockport, NY, 1977.
Foreword to *The Roses and the Windows*, by Rainer Maria Rilke, trans. A. Poulin Jr., Graywolf, Port Townsend, WA, 1979; reprinted in *The Complete French Poems of Rainer Maria Rilke*, trans. A. Poulin Jr., Graywolf, St. Paul, MN, 1986.
Foreword to *The Hardeman County Sequence*, by Michael Jennings, Heliographis, Rochester, 1980.
Foreword to *Un Ghimpe In Ininiu si Alte Poezii (Heart's Needle and Other Poems)*, trans. Ioan A. Popa, Editura Univers, Bucharest, 1983.
Introduction to *Leverage*, by Jonathan Holden, University of Virginia Press, Charlottesville, VA, 1983.
Introduction to *Dance Script for Electronic Ballerina*, by Alice Fulton, University of Pennsylvania Press, PA, 1983.
'Giving Up Music', *Syracuse Scholar* 5, no. 1, 1984, 69-78.
'Apple Trees and Belly Dancers, in *Singular Voices: American Poetry Today*, ed. Stephen Berg, Avon, New York, 1985.
'From the Journals of Woodchuck Charlie Robinson, Wilderness Guide and Trapper', *Bred*

Any Good Rooks Lately?, ed. James Charlton, Doubleday, Garden City, NY, 1986.
'The House of Snodgrass', 'Artist and Businessman', and 'Grandfathers and Sons', *Salmagundi* 78-79, Spring-Summer 1988, 176-205.
'Lutemaker is Real Craftsman' (Newspaper Headline), *Atencion*, San Miguel de Allende, Mexico, 12 February 1988.
'The Immutability of the Quick-Change Artist: Donald Hall', *The Day I Was Older: On the Poetry of Donald Hall*, ed. Liam Rector, Story Line, Santa Cruz, 1989.
'After-Images: Autobiographical Sketches', (I. Good House-keeping, II. Paralysis, III. Father), *The Southern Review* 25, no. 2, April 1989, 261-82.
'Against Your Beliefs', *The Southern Review* 26, no. 3, Summer 1990, 479-495.
'An Applecart Named Darwin', *Views* 3, no. 2, University of Louisville, 55-58.
Introduction to *Naming the Darkness*, by Jane Ellen Glasser, Road Publishers, Fairfax Station, VA, 1991.
'Pulse and Impulse', *The Southern Review* 27, no. 3, July 1991, 505-521.
'Shapes Merging and Emerging', *Shenandoah*, Winter 1991.
'Love And/Or War', *The Georgia Review*, XLVI, no. 1, Spring 1992, 97-112.
'Justice as Classmate', *Verse* 8, no. 3/9, no. 1, 1992, 14-15.
'A Liberal Education: Mentors, Fomenters and Tormentors', *The Southern Review*, 28, no. 3, Summer 1992, 445-468.
'Robert Hayden: The Man in the Middle', *Field* 47, Fall 1992, 20-30.
'Dabbling in Corruption', *The Paris Review* 36, no. 130, 1994, 201-213.
'Whitman's Selfsong', *The Southern Review* 32, no. 3, Summer 1996, 572-602.
Introduction to *The Education of Desire*, by William Dickey, Wesleyan University Press, 1996.
'Kathy's Blueberry Soup', *Lit à la carte: Favourite Recipes of Famous Authors*, comp. By Rex Beckham, Bay Side Press, Soquel, CA, 1996.
'In Response to the World of Del McGraw', in DeLoss McGraw, *As A Poem, So Is A Picture*, Scottsdale Center for the Arts, 1997, 13-32.

Interviews

Mahoney, Thomas, 'Pulitzer Poet Hits Stereotypes', *Ferndale Gazette-Times*, 5 May 1960, 1, 3.
Arnett, Judd, 'A Talk with a Poet: "Success is Hard to Digest"', *Detroit Free Press*, 8 May 1960.
Di Sesa, Debbie, 'Talking with a Poet: Meeting Snodgrass', *Daily Orange*, Syracuse University, 23 October 1964, 1.
Watson, Catherine, 'Snodgrass – Experience is Change', Minneapolis Sunday Tribune, 14 April 1968.
Anstett, Patricia, *Chicago Today Magazine*, 22 March 1970, 6-7.
Gerber, Philip L., and Gemmett, Robert, J., '"No Voices Talk to Me": A Conversation with W.D. Snodgrass', *Western Humanities Review* 24, Winter 1971, 61-71.
Popa, Ioan A., 'As sa vin din nou in Romania', *Tribuna* 16, no. 50, 14 December 1972, 8.
Boyers, Robert, 'W.D. Snodgrass: An Interview', *Salmagundi* 22-23, 1973, 149-63.
Gefen, Pearl Sheffy, 'The Strengths You Own', *Jerusalem Post Magazine*, 9 February 1973, 12.
Dillon, David, '"Toward Passionate Utterance": An Interview with W.D. Snodgrass', *Southwest Review* 60, no. 3, Summer 1975, 278-90; reprinted in *American Poetry Observed: Poets on their Work*, ed. Joe David Bellamy, University of Illinois Press, 1984.
Sollner, Werner, 'Nur Mich Selbst Ausdrucken', *Neue Literatur* 9, 1976, 61-63.
Packard, William, 'Craft Interview with W.D. Snodgrass', *New York Quarterly* 18, 1976; reprinted in *The Poet's Craft: Interviews from the 'New York Quarterly'*, ed. William

Packard, Paragon, NY, 1987.
Herz, Bob, 'An Interview with W.D. Snodgrass', *Seneca Review* 7, no. 2, December 1976.
Gaston, Paul L., 'W.D. Snodgrass and The Führer Bunker', *Papers on Language and Literature* 13, Summer 1977, 295-311, 13, Fall 1977, 401-12.
Niikura, Schinichi, 'Modern American Poet: An Interview with W.D. Snodgrass', *Modern Poetry Handbook* (Japan) 1, January 1978, 26-30.
Mathieu, Bertrand, 'Interview with W.D. Snodgrass', *Noiseless Spider*, University of New Haven, 8, no. 1, Fall 1978, 2-25.
Nickerson, Edward, A., 'Portrait of W.D. Snodgrass', *Delaware Today*, April 1983, 13-15.
Beacham, Walton, 'Richard Wilbur and W.D. Snodgrass: An Interview', *New Virginia Quarterly* 1, no. 1, 1979; reprinted in *Conversations with Richard Wilbur*, ed. William Butts, University of Mississippi Press, Jackson, MS, 1990.
Nelson, Greg, 'Interview with W.D. Snodgrass', *Phoebe: The George Mason Review* 14, Fall 1984, 30-42.
Vitale, Tom, *A Moveable Feast*, National Public Radio, WNYC, NY, 29 September 1987.
DeVries, Hillary, 'When Two Arts Interact: Poet W.D. Snodgrass and Artist DeLoss McGraw', *Christian Science Monitor*, 17 December 1987, 30-31.
Johnson, Bruce, 'Newark's Bearded Bard', *Delaware Today* 28, no. 2, February 1988.
Rosu, Dona, 'Dialog cu Poetal American W.D. Snodgrass', *Revista de Istorie so Teorie Literara* (Romania) 36, nos. 3-4, July-December 1988, 281-288.
Di Angelo, Mary Jo, 'W.D. Snodgrass', *University of Delaware Magazine* 1, no. 3, Spring 1989, 30-35.
Raisor, Philip, 'Framed Portrait: An Interview with W.D. Snodgrass', *The Southern Review* 26, no. 1, January 1990, 65-80.
Spires, Elizabeth, 'W. D. Snodgrass: An Interview', *American Poetry Review* 19, no. 4, July/August 1990, 38-46.
Haven, Stephen, 'An Interview with W.D. Snodgrass: Recent Work', *Crazyhorse*, Spring 1990, 76-92.
Patrick, William, 'An Interview with W.D. Snodgrass', *Dominion Review* 11, Spring 1993, 42-69.
Hasty, Charles, 'W.D. Snodgrass: An Interview', *San Miguel Writer* 7, Summer 1993, 11-35.
Lyons, Art, 'W.D. Snodgrass: An Interview', *High Plains Literary Review* 3, no. 2, Fall 1993, 128-138.
Eyle, Alexandra, 'Interview with W.D. Snodgrass', *The Paris Review* 36, no. 130, 1994, 165-200.

Recordings

Videotapes

A Poet in Radical Pursuit, recorded by Alexandra Eyle, Syracuse, 1986.
The Poetry of W.D. Snodgrass, The Brockport Writers' Forum, SUNY, Brockport.
W.D. Snodgrass: Pulitzer Prize Winning Poet, Mount Union College Convocation Series, 10 April 1997.

Audiotapes

National Poetry Festival, Library of Congress, Washington, D.C., 1962.

Twentieth-Century Poetry in English: John Ciardi and W.D. Snodgrass, Library of Congress, Washington, D.C., 1962.
Calling from the Wood's Edge, Watershed Tapes, Washington, D.C., 1985.
Poets for Peace, Spoken Arts, New Rochelle, New York.
Spoken Arts Treasury of 100 Modern Poets, Spoken Arts, New Rochelle, New York.

Theatrical and Musical Productions

Biedermann and the Firebugs, by Max Frisch, trans. and adapted by W.D. Snodgrass and Rosemarie Waldrop, dir. David Hamilton, Regent Theater, Syracuse University, 29-30 April, 1 May 1966.
The Führer Bunker: A Cycle of Poems in Progress, staged by Paul Dicklin, Roverview Playhouse, Old Dominion University, Norfolk, VA, 27 September 1978.
Dr Joseph Goebbels, 22 April 1945, performed with percussion in concert, West Gate Theater, New York, 6-7 November 1981.
The Führer Bunker, adapted by W.D. Snodgrass, dir. Carl Weber, American Place Theater, New York, April-June 1981.
The Führer Bunker, adapted and dir. Gary Fisher, Buffalo Entertainment Theater, 23 September 1982.
The Führer Bunker, adapted by W.D. Snodgrass and Annette Martin, dir. Annette Martin, Eastern Michigan State University, Ypsilanti, MI, 3-11 April 1987.
Midnight Carnival, Faustwork Mask Theater, dir. Wynn Handman, American Place Theatre, New York, 5-16 December 1990.
'Song Translations by W.D. Snodgrass', performed by Agnes Fuller, Frank Ward, and the Old Dominium Collegium Musicum, directed by Lee Teply, October 5 1992: 'Reis de Bornelh', by Giraut de Bornelh, 'Escotaz, mas no say que ses', by Raimbaut d'Orange, 'A l'entrada del tens clar', Anon. (13th Cent.), 'Nach der senenden claghe', by Wizlav von Rugen, 'Toda mi vida os ame', by Luis Milan, 'L'autr'ier jost una sebissa', by Marcabrun, 'Qui veut chasser une migraine', by Gabriel Bataille, 'Dale si le das', Anon. (c.1500), 'Se l'aura spira', by Girolamo Frescobaldo, 'Chi la gagliarda', by Giovanni Domenico da Nola, 'Tanzen und Springen', by Hans Leo Hassler.

– Forthcoming –

Translations

Selected Translations, BOA Editions, Brockport, New York, 1998.

Criticism

To Sound Like Yourself

Memoirs

After-Images

Secondary Works

Books

Gaston, Paul L., *W.D. Snodgrass*, Twayne, Boston, 1978.
Ed. Haven, Stephen, *The Poetry of W.D. Snodgrass: Everything Human*, University of Michigan Press, Ann Arbor, MI, 1993. (A comprehensive selection of book reviews and critical essays, with contributions from Philip Booth, William Dickey, John Hollander, Louis Simpson, Judson Jerome, M.L. Rosenthal, Hayden Carruth, W.W. Robson, Donald Davie, Gilbert Sorrentino, George Monteiro, Denis Donoghue, Stanley Moss, Josephine Jacobsen, Clive James, Robert Boyers, William Heyen, Richard Howard, Robert Phillips, J.D. McClatchy, Richard Horwich, Michael Wood, Harold Bloom, Peter L. Simpson, Robert Peters, Hugh Kenner, Dana Gioia, Gavin Ewart, Wayne Koestenbaum, Robert McDowell, Larry Levis, Gertrude M. White, David Wojahn, Richard Jackson, Leslie Ullman, Laurence Goldstein, Donald Hall, Robert Dana, X.J. Kennedy.)
Weigel, Molly, *The Leonard L. Milberg Collection of American Poetry*, Princeton University Press, Princeton, NJ, 327-333. (A commentary on Snodgrass's career, together with a bibliography of the library's holdings of work by Snodgrass.)

Articles

Lyttle, David, 'Snodgrass Walking', *Approach* 41, Fall 1961, 13-16.
Ed. Moritz, Charles, *Current Biography 1960*, Wilson, New York, 1961.
'People on the Way Up', *Saturday Evening Post* 235, no. 22, 2 June 1962, 26.
Torchiana, Donald T., 'Heart's Needle: Snodgrass Strides through the Universe', *TriQuarterly* 2, Spring 1960, 18-26; reprinted in ed. Hungerford, Edward B., *Poets in Progress: Critical Prefaces to Thirteen Modern American Poets*, Northwestern University Press, Evanston, IL, 1962.
Monteiro, George, 'Snodgrass Peoples His Universe', *Papers of the Bibliographical Society of America* 56, no. 4, 1962, 494-495.
Barolini, Antonio, 'Una Poeta Americano', Il Mondo, 3 December 1963, 11.
White, William, 'Snodgrass Peoples His Universe: II', *Papers of the Bibliographical Society of America* 57, no. 1, 1963, 94.
Farrelly, David, 'Heart's Fling: The Poetry of W.D. Snodgrass', *Perspective* 13, Winter 1964, 185-199.
Mavor, Ronald, 'An American Poet Steals the Show', *The Scotsman* (Edinburgh), 26 August 1965, 6.
Ed. Shaw, John MacKay, *Childhood in Poetry*, Gale, Detroit, 1967.
Carroll, Paul, 'The Thoreau Complex amid the Solid Scholars', in *The Poem and its Skin*, Follett, Chicago & New York, 1968, 174-187.
Phillips, Robert, 'W.D. Snodgrass and the Sad Hospital of the World', *University of Windsor Review* 4, no. 2, Spring 1969; reprinted in *The Confessional Poets*, Southern Illinois University Press, Carbondale and Edwardsville, 1973.
Heyen, William, 'Fishing the Swamp: The Poetry of W.D. Snodgrass', in ed. Mazzaro, Jerome, *Modern American Poetry: Essays in Criticism*, McKay, New York, 1970.

Eds. Bradbury, Malcolm, et al, *Penguin Companion to American Literature*, McGraw, New York, 1971.

Mazzaro, Jerome, 'The Public Intimacy of W.D. Snodgrass', *Salmagundi* 19, Spring 1972, 96-111.

McClatchy, J.D., 'W.D.Snodgrass: The Mild Reflective Art', *Massachusetts Review* 16, Spring 1975, 281-314; reprinted in *White Paper: On Contemporary American Poetry*, Columbia University Press, New York, 1989.

Cantrell, Carol Helmstetter, 'Self and Tradition in Recent Poetry', *Midwest Quarterly* 18, 1977, 343-360.

Seulean, Joan, 'Romanian Ballads Translated into English', *Romanian Bulletin* 7, January 1978, 11-12.

Hoffman, Stephen K., 'Impersonal Personalism: The Making of a Confessional Poet', *ELH* 45, no. 4, Winter 1978, 687-707.

Curtis, Simon, 'Recent Poetry', *Critical Quarterly* 21, no. 2, 1979, 75-84.

White, Gertrude M., 'To Tell the Truth: The Poems of W.D. Snodgrass', *Odyssey* 3, no. 2, 1979, 10-18.

Eds. Bede, Jean-Albert, and Edterton, William B., *Columbia Dictionary of Modern European Literature*, 2nd ed., Columbia University Press, New York, 1980.

Helterman, Jeffrey, 'W.D. Snodgrass', in ed. Greiner, Donald J., *Dictionary of Literary Biography: American Poets since World War II*, Gale, Detroit, 1980.

Howard, Richard, 'There's Something Beats the Same in Opposed Hearts', in *Alone with America*, Atheneum, New York, 1980, 548-561.

Berke, Roberta, In *Bounds out of Bound: A Compass for Recent American and British Poetry*, 81-85, Oxford University Press, New York, 1981.

Popa, Ioan A, 'Intre Folclor si Poezia Moderna', *Contemporanul* (Romania) 35, 27 August 1982, 16.

Williams, Edwin W., 'W.D. Snodgrass', in ed. Magill, Frank N., *Survey of Poetry: English Language Series*, Vol. 6, Salem, Englewood Cliffs, NJ, 1982.

Miller, Elsie, 'The Artist and the Poet', *San Diego Magazine* 35, no. 11, September 1983, 146-151.

Vreeland, Susan, 'Painter as Poet: The McGraw-Snodgrass Connection', *Hill Courier* (San Diego) 2, no. 7, August 1984, 12-13.

Survey of American Poetry, Vol. 10, Roth, Great Neck, 1984.

Milburn, Michael, '"Sacred Beings": Writers in Recorded Conversation', *Poetry* 146, no. 2, 1985, 101-111.

Mah, Marsha, and Foltz, Lyn, 'Success Secrets', *Delaware Today* 25, no. 12, December 1986, 65.

Leary, Robyn, 'Pulitzer Prize-Winning Poet at University of Delaware', *Delaware State News*, 3 July 1988.

Goldstein, Lawrence, 'The Führer Bunker and the New Discourse about Nazism', *Southern Review* 24, no. 1, Winter 1988, 100-114.

Who's Who in America, 46th ed., 1989-1990.

Gray, Richard, *American Poetry of the Twentieth Century*, Longman, London and New York, 1990, 227-229.

'UD Professor Full of Rhyme, Reason', *News Journal* (Wilmington DE), 21 May 1991, A11.

Vourvoulias, Sabrina, 'Pulitzer Winning Poet Summers in Chenango Valley', *Chenango Valley News*, 26 July 1991, 7.

Soulsman, Gary, 'UD Poet Recalls Anne Sexton's Mania', *Sunday News Journal*, Wilmington, DE, 15 December 1991.

Raban, Jonathan, 'Snodgrass, W.D.' entry in ed. Hamilton, Ian, *Oxford Companion to Twentieth-Century Poetry*, Oxford University Press, 1994, 504-505.

Journals

'Poetry Society of AmericaTribute to the *American Poetry Review*: Armand Schwerner, W. D. Snodgrass, and Ann Waldman', *PSA News* 43, Winter 1994, 24.
Agenda 34, no. 1, 'A Tribute to W.D. Snodgrass', Spring 1996. (With essays by James Fenton, Philip Hoy, Pete Smith, Michael Collier.)

Reviews

Heart's Needle

Dickey, William, *Epoch* 9, Spring 1959, 254-256.
Booth, Philip, *Christian Science Monitor*, 14 May 1959.
Holmes, John, *Saturday Review* 42, 23 May 1959, 21+.
Picton, John, *Vancouver Sun*, 23 May 1959.
Farina, Richard G., *Cornell Daily Sun*, 28 May 1959.
Robie, B.A., *Library Journal* 84, 1 June 1959, 1897.
Hall, Donald, *New York Herald Tribune Book Review* 35, 19 July 1959, 3.
Meredith, William, *New York Times Book Review* 64, 26 July 1959, 25.
Fiscalini, Janet, *Commonweal* 70, 14 August 1959, 429-430.
Hohler, Dayton, *Louisville Courier Journal*, 17 August 1959.
Fasel, Ida, *Wichita Falls Times – Feature Magazine*, 6 September 1959, 7.
Hollander, John, *Partisan Review* 26, no. 3, Summer 1959, 503.
Virginia Quarterly Review 33, Summer 1959, cxxx.
Simpson, Louis, *The Hudson Review* 12, no. 2, Summer 1959, 308.
Thompson, John, *Kenyon Review* 21, no. 3, Summer 1959, 488-490.
Bogan, Louise, *New Yorker* 35, 24 October 1959, 196.
Rosenthal, M.L., *Nation* 189, 24 October 1959, 257-258.
Bakhash, Alfred K., *Audience* 6, no. 4, Autumn 1959, 103-108.
Carruth, Hayden, *Poetry* 95, no. 2, November 1959, 118-121.
Jerome, Judson, *Antioch Review* 19, Fall 1959, 429-432.
Legler, Philip, *New Mexico Quarterly* 29, 1959, 449.
Book Review Digest, January 1960.
Turco, Lewis, *Voices*, January-April 1960, 47-50.
Hoffman, Daniel G., *Sewanee Review* 68, no. 1, Winter 1960, 122-123.
Church Times (England), 17 February 1961.
Davie, Donald, *Spectator* 206, 24 March 1961, 416.
Robson, W.W., *The Observer*, 12 March 1961, 28.
Furbank, P.N., *Listener*, 30 March 1961, 583.
Times Literary Supplement, 7 April 1961, 218.
Hamilton, Ian, *Oxford Opinion* 47, 8 May 1961, 28.
Thompson, Frank, *Prairie Schooner* 35, no. 2, June 1961, 182.
Skelton, Robin, *Critical Quarterly* 3, no. 2, Summer 1961, 187.
Sorrentino, Gilbert, *Yugen* 7, 1961, 5-7.

Kliatt Young Adult Paperback Book Guide 18, Spring 1984, 29.

Gallows Songs

Seymour-Smith, Martin, *Spectator* 221, 6 September 1968, 328-329.

After Experience

Kirkus Review 35, 15 December 1967, 1519.
Publishers Weekly 192, 25 December 1967, 54.
Layton, R.F., *Library Journal* 93, 15 January 1968, 193.
Book Review Digest, January 1968.
Geran, Juliana, *Maroon* (Chicago), 1 March 1968.
News-Leader (Richmond, VA), 20 March 1968.
Lask, Thomas, *New York Times*, 30 March 1968, 31.
Worcester, Massachusetts Telegram, 31 March 1968.
Johnson, R.P., *Minneapolis Tribune*, 14 April 1968.
Walsh, Chad, *Washington Post Book World*, 14 April 1968, 6.
Smith, Ray, *Minneapolis Star*, 19 April 1968.
Donoghue, Denis, *The New York Review of Books* 10, 25 April 1968, 17.
Beall, DeWitt, *Chicago News*, 27 April 1968.
Harrison, J., *The New York Times Book Review* 73, 28 April 1968, 6.
Booklist 64, 1 May 1968, 1018.
Brady, Charles A., *Buffalo News*, 18 May 1968.
Pearre, Howell, *Nashville Banner*, 24 May 1968.
Howes, Victor, *Christian Science Monitor*, 29 May 1968, 11.
Jerome, Judson, *Saturday Review* 51, 1 June 1968, 32.
Dickey, R.P., *Missourian* (Columbia), 2 June 1968.
Moss, S., *New Republic* 158, 15 June 1968, 35.
Jacobsen, J., *Commonweal* 88, 21 June 1968, 417.
Leibowitz, Herbert, *The Hudson Review* 21, no. 3, August 1968, 553.
Simpson, Louis, *Harper's* 237, August 1968, 74.
Mazzaro, Jerome, *Nation* 207, 16 September 1968, 252.
Conarroe, Joel, *Shenandoah* 19, no. 4, Summer 1968, 77-88.
Hine, Daryl, *Poetry* 113, October 1968, 52.
Lieberman, L., *Yale Review* 58, Autumn 1968, 137.
Virginia Quarterly Review 44, Summer 1968, ciii.
Bogan Louise, *The New Yorker* 44, 28 December 1968, 63.
Martz, William, *December 10*, no. 1, 1968, 197.
Porter, Peter, *London Magazine* 8, no. 12, 1968, 85-87.
Twentieth Century 176, no. 1039, 1968, 90.
James, Clive, *Times Literary Supplement*, 2 January 1969, 7; reprinted in James, Clive, *The Metropolitan Critic*, Faber, London, 1974, 112-116.
Kavanagh, P.J., *The Guardian Weekly* 101, 2 January 1969, 15.
Brownjohn, Alan, *New Statesman* 77, 10 January 1969, 52.
Homberger, Eric, *Cambridge Review*, 17 January 1969, 206.
Dodsworth, Martin, *Listener* 81, 27 March 1969, 433.
Dale, Peter, *Agenda* 7, no. 2, Spring 1969, 79-81.
Boyers, Robert, *Partisan Review* 36, no. 2, 1969, 306.

Swenson, May, *The Southern Review* 7, 1971, 954.

Remains

Heyen, William, *Western Humanities Review* 25, no. 3, Summer 1971, 253-256.
Phillips, Robert, *Poet Lore* 68, no. 1, Spring 1973, 102-106.

In Radical Pursuit

Kirkus Review 42, 15 September 1974, 1051.
Isaacson, David, *Library Journal* 99, 1 October 1974, 2482.
Publishers Weekly 206, 25 November 1974, 41.
Horwich, Richard, *New Republic* 172, 15 February 1975, 31.
Booklist 71, 1 April 1975, 787.
Wood, Michael, *The New York Review of Books* 22, 17 April 1975, 15.
Choice 12 , May 1975, 387.
Hall, Donald, *American Poetry Review* 4, May-June 1975, 28.
White, Gertrude M., *Criticism* 17, Fall 1975, 373-375.
Atlas, James, *American Poetry Review* 5, March 1976, 35.
Fisher, Benjamin Franklin IV, *American Book Collector* 26, March-April 1976, 4.
Yale Review 65, no. 3, Spring 1976, viii-vix.
Daniel, Robert W., *Sewanee Review* 84, Summer 1976, xc-xciii .
Asselineau, Roger, *Études Anglaises* 31, nos. 3-4, 1978, 423-424.

The Führer Bunker: A Cycle of Poems in Progress

Chicago Daily News, 27 August 1977.
Rochester Democrat and Chronicle, 1 September 1977.
Bloom, Harold, *New Republic* 177, 26 November 1977, 25.
San Francisco Review of Books, November 1977.
Peters, Robert, *American Book Review* 1, December 1977, 13; reprinted in *The Great American Poetry Bake-Off*, Scarecrow Press, Metuchen, NJ and London, 1979.
Library Journal 102, 15 December 1977, 2166.
Simpson, Peter L., *St. Louis Post-Dispatch*, 20 December 1977, 3B.
Small Press Bookclub, Christmas 1977.
Fremont-Smith, Eliot, *Village Voice* 22, 26 December 1977, 75.
Publishers Weekly, 26 December 1977.
Keith, Harrison, *Carleton Miscellany* 17, Winter 1977-1978, 147.
Kenner, Hugh, *New York Times Book Review*, 1 January 1978, 11.
Choice 14, January 1978, 1499.
Booklist 74, 15 April 1978, 1321.
Cotter, J.F., *The Hudson Review* 31, Spring 1978, 212.
North American Review 1, Spring 1978.
Quest, May-June 1978.
Yenser, Stephen, *Yale Review* 68, no. 5, Fall 1978, 86-90.
Morris, John N., *Ohio Review* 19, no. 1, Winter 1978, 110-112.
Asselineau, Roger, *Études Anglaises* 31, nos. 3-4, 1978, 424.
Selzer, David, *Poetry Review* (England) 67, no. 4, 1978, 49-51.
Stony Hills 4, no. 2, 1978.

Von Hallberg, Robert, *Chicago Review* 31, no. 3, Winter 1980, 116-120.

Six Troubadour Songs

Bloom, Harold, *New Republic* 177, 26 November 1977, 26.
American Book Review 1, December 1977, 14.
Booklist 74, 15 December 1977, 663-664.
Library Journal 102, 15 December 1977, 2473.
Kenner, Hugh, *New York Times Book Review*, 1 January 1978, 11.
Choice 15, March 1978, 80.
Virginia Quarterly Review 54, Spring 1978, 58.
Carruth, Hayden, *The Hudson Review* 31, Summer 1978, 383.
Harrison, Keith, *Carleton Miscellany* 17, Spring 1979, 234.

If Birds Build with Your Hair

Gioia, Dana, *The Hudson Review* 35, Autumn 1982, 483.

Selected Poems: 1957-1987

Stuttaford, Genevieve, *Publishers Weekly*, 2 June 1987.
Roffman, Rosaly DeMaios, *Library Journal* 112, August 1987, 130.
Ewart, Gavin, *New York Times Book Review*, 13 September 1987, 52.
Harris, Jana, *Seattle Times*, 18 October 1987.
Pinson, Ernest, *Jackson Sun* (Jackson, TN), 1 November 1987, C4.
Koestenbaum, Wayne, *Village Voice* 32, no. 46, 17 November 1987, 63.
Bawer, Bruce, *Washington Post Book World*, 3 January 1988.
Goldgar, Harry, *St. Petersburg Times*, 3 January 1988.
Geier, A. Woodrow, *Sunday Tennessean*, 27 March 1988, 9F.
Laizik, S., and Bing, Mark, *Philadelphia Inquirer*, 6 March 1988, F3.
Jerome, Judson, *Writer's Digest*, March 1988, 13.
Hall, Donald, *Partisan Review* 55, Summer 1988, 505-507.
Virginia Quarterly Review 64, no. 3, Summer 1988, 98.
McGovern, Martin, *Houston Post*, 17 January 1988.
McDuff, David, *Stand* 29, Autumn 1988, 66-67.
McDowell, Robert, *The Hudson Review* 40, no. 4, Winter 1988, 677-685.
Gwynn, R.S., *Dictionary of Literary Biography: 1987*, ed. J.M. Brook, Gale, Detroit, 1988.
Levis, Larry, *American Poetry Review* 18, no. 1, January-February 1989, 9-14.
Lovelock, Yann, *Oasis* 38 (England), January 1990.
Logan, William, *Parnassus* 16, no. 1, Summer 1990, 72-86.

W.D.'s Midnight Carnival

'Word and Image at Play', *This World (San Francisco Chronicle)*, 30 October 1988, 10-11.

The Death of Cock Robin

Virginia Quarterly Review, Summer 1990, 100-101.

Chappell, Fred, *Georgia Review* 45, Summer 1991, 383-394.

Each In His Season

Bennett, Bruce, 'On the Seamy Side of the Street', *The New York Times Book Review*, 17 April 1994.
Jacob, John, *Small Press* 12, no. 2, Spring 1994.
Pratt, William, *World Literature Today*, Spring 1994.
Slavitt, David, R., 'How Much Is a Poem Worth?: Appreciating W.D. Snodgrass', *Seven Arts*, July 1994.
Irving, Augusta, '... In His Season', *Atencion*, San Miguel de Allende, Mexico, 20, no. 20, p. 2.
Aimone, Joseph, *Hellas* 6, no. 1, Spring/Summer 1995, 139-141.
Malin, Irving, *Texas Review*, 1995.

The Fuehrer Bunker: The Complete Cycle

Allen, Frank, *Library Journal*, 1 April 1995.
Guenther, Charles, 'Hitler's Last Days', *St Louis Post Dispatch*, 2 April 1995.
Susskind, Harriet, 'The Final Chapter', *Democrat and Chronicle*, Rochester, NY, 9 April 19-95.
Gunderson, Elizabeth, *Booklist*, Spring 1995.
Morris, Bernard E., *The Harvard Review* 9, November 1995.
Murphy, Kay, *Chelsea*, January 1996.

Theatrical Productions

Barnes, Clive, *New York Post*, 3 June 1981, 16.
Gussow, Mel, *New York Times*, 3 June 1981, C21.
Wynne, Peter, *Record*, 3 June 1981.
Kissel, Howard, *Women's Wear Daily*, 4 June 1981.
Raidy, William A., *Star Ledger*, 4 June 1981.
Evans, Jeremy, *Show Business*, 10 June 1981.
Feingold, Michael, *Village Voice*, 10-16 June 1981, 93-94.
Gilman, Richard, *Nation*, 27 June 1981, 803-804.
Sauvage, Leo, *New Leader* 64, no. 13, 1981, 22.
Post-Standard (Syracuse, NY), 30 April 1986, 7.
Eastern Echo (Ypsilanti, MI), 1 April 1987, 5.
Ann Arbor News, 7 April 1987, D5.

Dissertations

Blankenburg, Gary Dean, *A Rhetorical Approach to Confessional Poetry: Plath, Sexton, Lowell, Berryman and Snodgrass*, Carnegie-Mellon, 1983, University of Michigan Press, Ann Arbor, MI, 1984, 84-06438.
Goodman, Diane Beth, '"Heart's Needle": A Guide to the Original Manuscript', Case Western Reserve, 1989.
McClatchy, J. D., *Bloody-Hot and Personal: The Tradition of Contemporary Confessional Poetry*, Yale, 1974, University of Michigan Press, Ann Arbor, MI, 1975, 75-15336.

Bibliographies

Gaston, Paul L., 'Selected Bibliography', W.D. Snodgrass, 167-170, Twayne, Boston, 1978.
White, William, *W.D. Snodgrass: A Bibliography*, Wayne State University, Detroit, 1960.
Snodgrass, Kathleen, with DeNiord, Chard, W.D. Snodgrass Bibliography, in ed. Stephen Haven, *The Poetry of W.D. Snodgrass: Everything Human*, University of Michigan Press, Ann Arbor MI, 1993, 305-315.

– Forthcoming –

Ed. Raisor, Philip, *Tuned and Under Tension: The Recent Poetry of W.D. Snodgrass* (with essays by Zack Bowen, Bernard Benstock, Fred Chappell, Anne Colwell, Devon Miller-Duggan, Peter Makuck, David Metzger, Philip Raisor, and an interview by Beth Tremblay).

The Snodgrass Archives

With one exception, all of Snodgrass's early manuscripts are held by the library of the University of Buffalo, Buffalo, New York. The exception is the manuscript of *Heart's Needle*, which, together with Snodgrass's later manuscripts, is held by the library of the University of Delaware, Newark, Delaware.

The Critics

'I had a boy last summer at Colorado who was good (did an excellent Rilke translation) and most of his poems were excellent though unconscious imitations of you. You'd had him in a class at Iowa, I think – DeWitt Snodgrass, poor ill-named one!'

Randall Jarrell, letter to Robert Lowell, November 1951.

'I must tell you that I've discovered a new poet, W.D. Snodgrass – he was once one of my Iowa students, and I merely thought him about the best. Now he turns out to be better than anyone, except Larkin.'

Robert Lowell, letter to Elizabeth Bishop, 1957

'I have been writing very hard myself lately and have written almost half a book since the middle of August, and feel I have just really begun to know how to get out what I want to say, what I've lived. You learned earlier.'

Robert Lowell, letter to W.D. Snodgrass, 1957

'Snodgrass recognizes the main task of the poet: to tell the truth and avoid falsifying. He has put on no fine masks to which his features must hereafter conform; he is free to develop.'

Louis Simpson, review of *Heart's Needle*, 1959

'In my mind the question raises itself whether or not the poems should have been published at all. This is not simply a matter of propriety, but of the warping sentimentality that is engendered in the recording of experience so little transmuted from private specificity.'

Hayden Carruth, discussing the title sequence in a review of *Heart's Needle*, 1959

'I don't like Snodgrass: dopy kid-mad sod. Poetic Salinger.'

Philip Larkin, letter to Anthony Thwaite, 1961

'No, confound it, it's my friends who are wrong: self-pity, self-esteem, all sorts of self-regard, are fatal to poetry – and most of the poems in *Heart's Needle* are self-regarding. A poem is not the public parade of a private emotion; however smoothly executed, such para-

dings belong elsewhere than in the blessedly impersonal art of poetry.'

Donald Davie, review of *Heart's Needle*, 1961

'A poet in a country where anything can be turned in for a new one, W.D. Snodgrass stays loyal to his unpoetic surname, and the essential claim his poetry makes is that it is necessary to write beautifully.'

Clive James, review of *After Experience*, 1969

'It seems to me that this sequence is at least as fine as Snodgrass's 'Heart's Needle' and, as such, deserves high praise indeed. It may be, in fact, that its effect is even stronger.'

William Heyen, review of *Remains*, 1971.

'It's a pleasure to report ... that, when W.D. Snodgrass turns from poetry ... to criticism, he serves up a veritable banquet, full of nourishment and taste.'

Richard Horwich, review of *In Radical Pursuit*, 1975

'I admire the impulse behind Snodgrass's essays a good deal – he wishes to connect literature with the most familiar and unknown (unknown because familiar) experiences of daily life – but the essays themselves issue too often in helpless, narrow simplicities.'

Michael Wood, review of *In Radical Pursuit*, 1975

'I started reading this [book] with anticipated dread and distaste, though with admiration for Snodgrass's audacity. His audacity is more than matched by his astonishing skill in ordering his intractable material and in combining his own inventions with the verifiable details of the last days of Hitler. Granted the immense difficulties he has taken on, Snodgrass demonstrates something of the power of a contemporary equivalent of Jacobean drama at its darkest.'

Harold Bloom, review of *The Führer Bunker:
A Cycle of Poems in Progress*, 1977

'Why Snodgrass should be wasting his gift on attempts to outdo 'the banality of evil' I can't begin to guess.'

Hugh Kenner, review of *The Führer Bunker:
A Cycle of Poems in Progress*, 1978

'Snodgrass's project is audacious enough to keep most poets from giving it a second thought, but it has given him an occasion to which his passionate curiosity about human nature, his architectonic powers, his prosodic finesse, and his evident capacity for research allow him to rise.'

> Stephen Yenser, review of *The Führer Bunker:*
> *A Cycle of Poems in Progress*, 1978

'...Snodgrass is not ... as well and favourably known as he ought to be. The reason, I think, lies in his most striking characteristic: his resolute, uncompromising, almost frightening honesty ... Snodgrass's verse tells the truth, however painful to himself or to others. It neither fakes, evades, exhibits ego for the sake of exhibitionism, nor grinds the axe of fad or ideology. It demonstrates what he himself has declared to be requisite for the 'terribly hard work that writing is ... a complete removal from any ulterior motive, an absolute dedication to the object and the experience."

> Gertrude M. White, 'To Tell the Truth: The Poems of
> W.D. Snodgrass', 1979

'On the evidence of his *Selected Poems 1957-87* W.D. Snodgrass is one of the six best poets now writing in English ...'

> Gavin Ewart, review of *Selected Poems* 1957-8, 1987

'This master inspires reverence.'

> Wayne Koestenbaum, review of *Selected Poems 1957-87*, 1987

'Readers of this book ... will discover poem after poem with integrity's weight in them. We do not much associate integrity with poetry anymore. But I must use the word here. Like Yeats, Snodgrass writes a formal poetry of aggression that challenges our smug conventions and asks us to be wiser, more humane.'

> Robert McDowell, review of *Selected Poems 1957-1987*, 1988

'The best of the poems in [this book] are so central to our lives and our thought that I think they should be read by anyone interested in poetry at all.'

> Larry Levis, review of *Selected Poems 1957-87*, 1989

'It is not difficult to believe W.D. Snodgrass's boast that he is descended, on one side of his family, from Robert Herrick and, on the other, from Robert Burns. His lyricism is not only the most consistent among the confessional poets, it is the most insistent ...'

J.D. McClatchy, 'W.D. Snodgrass: The Mild Reflective Art', 1989

'With a few exceptions, like the bravura 'A Darkling Alphabet,' these latest poems are not only a disappointment but a puzzle: Why would a poet with such gifts, even in his search for diversity and new 'voices,' deliberately parody those gifts and wreck a career?'

J.D. McClatchy, discussing *The Death of Cock Robin* in
'W.D. Snodgrass: The Mild Reflective Art', 1989

'The volume is a Cartier's window of prosodic forms of every sort, and most of them are handled with ... ebullience and aplomb ... via lines that draw much of their energy from nursery rhymes and other folk and popular sources ... It goes without saying that there is metrical and rhyming ingenuity aplenty.'

Fred Chappell, review of *The Death of Cock Robin*, 1991

'I could not possibly exaggerate the importance of Snodgrass for me and many another writer back in those Dark Ages when Ginsberg's *Howl* was heard across the land, drowning out other voices, and when poets in droves were deserting the apparently sinking ship of traditional form.'

X.J. Kennedy, 'The Size of Snodgrass', 1993

'Like Penelope, Snodgrass unravels everything he weaves in order to reweave within new patterns and frames, which makes a collection like this recent one far more than the sum of its parts (some old, most new, nothing borrowed, decidedly blue).'

Bernard Benstock, discussing *Each in His Season* in
'A Poet for All Seasons', 1996

Between The Lines

Other volumes currently in preparation:

Hans Magnus Enzensberger
in conversation with Philip Hoy

Donald Hall
in conversation with Ian Hamilton

Michael Hamburger
in conversation with Peter Dale

Anthony Hecht
in conversation with Philip Hoy

Anthony Thwaite
in conversation with Peter Dale and Ian Hamilton

Richard Wilbur
in conversation with Peter Dale

For further information, please contact:

Between The Lines

9 Woodstock Road,
London N4 3ET,
UK.

Tel: 44 (0)171-272 8719

Fax: 44 (0)181-374 5736

e-mail: philiphoy@aol.com

Or visit our website:

http://www.pbk.co.uk/btl/